ALL HOPE IS GONE

Music transcriptions by Pete Billmann and David Stocker

ISBN 978-1-4234-6505-8

7777 W. BLUEMOUND RD. P.O. BOX 13819 MILWAUKEE, WI 53213

In Australia Contact:
Hal Leonard Australia Pty. Ltd.
4 Lentara Court
Cheltenham, Victoria, 3192 Australia
Email: ausadmin@halleonard.com.au

Visit Hal Leonard Online at
www.halleonard.com

.Execute.

Words and Music by Slipknot

Drop D tuning, down 1 1/2 steps:
(low to high) B-F♯-B-E-G♯-C♯

Free time

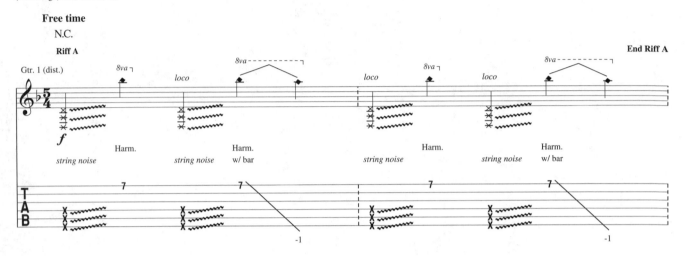

Gtr. 1: w/ Riff A (till end)

Spoken: It appears that we have reached the edge, that zenith where stimuli and comatose collide. Forty years ago, The Man proclaimed the Age of the Gross to be upon us, and even though The Man was destroying our heritage and insulting our intelligence, that era has become very real. We labor for pleasure and abhor the guilt of pressure. My generation will go down as the architects of contemporary disgust. Some have fought and died. Others have allowed the strong to be butchered for a price they themselves don't care about and will never understand. I myself am beleaguered by the selfish face of a kind of man that is not Mankind. Distrust in information.

Fundamentalism of opinion. Catastrophic boredom and a fanatical devotion to that which does not matter.

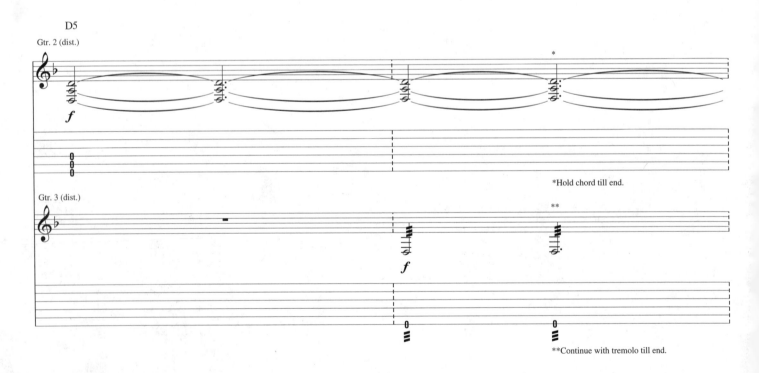

Where is your glory now, people? Where are your gods and politicians? Where is your shame and salvation? You rage for no reason because you have no reason. What have you ever fought for? What have you ever bled for? The face of the Earth is scarred with the walking dead. The Age of the Gross is a living virus. This is the future you have created. This is the world you have set ablaze. All your lies are coming true. All freedom is lost. All hope is gone.

Gematria (The Killing Name)

Words and Music by Slipknot

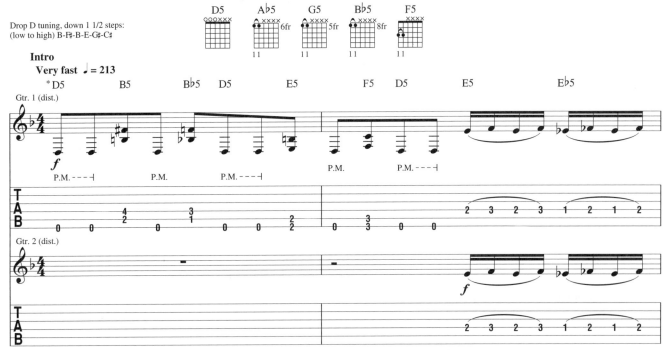

Drop D tuning, down 1 1/2 steps:
(low to high) B-F♯-B-E-G♯-C♯

Intro
Very fast ♩ = 213

*Chord symbols reflect implied harmony.

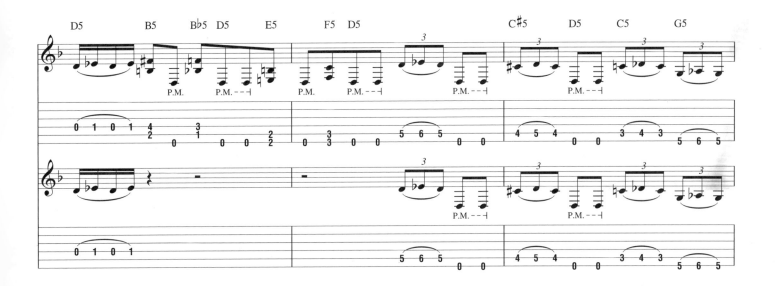

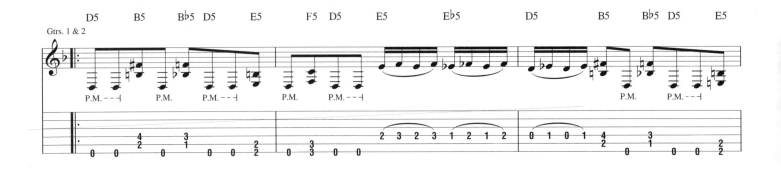

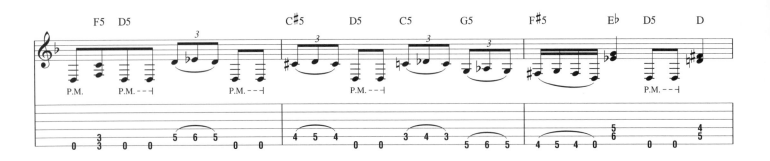

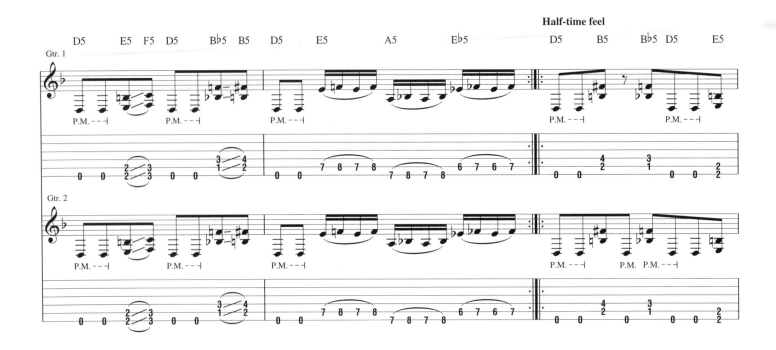

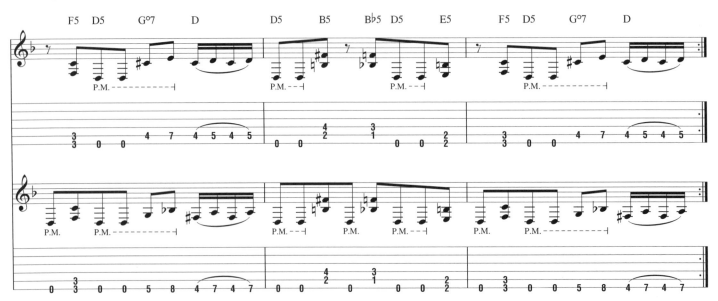

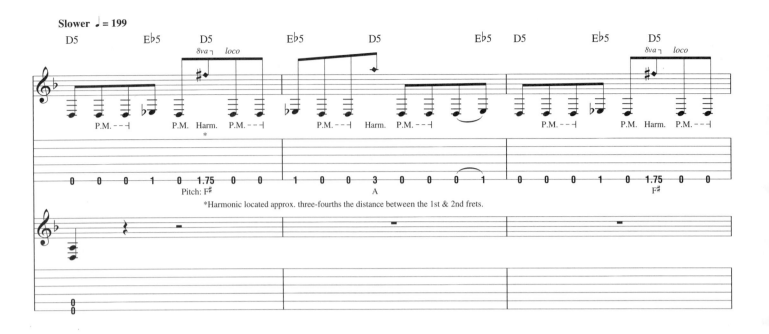

*Harmonic located approx. three-fourths the distance between the 1st & 2nd frets.

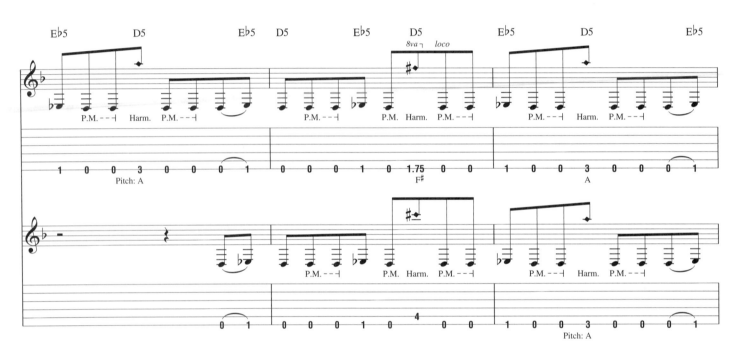

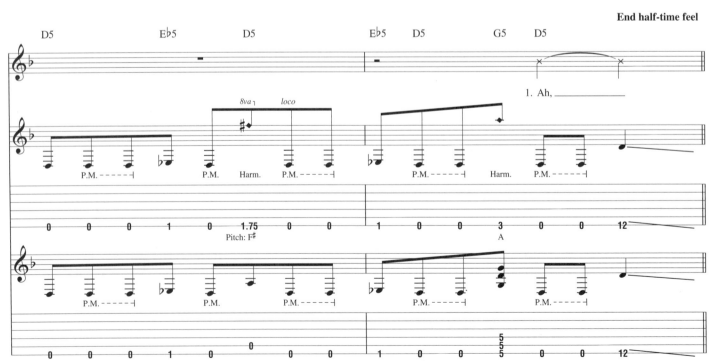

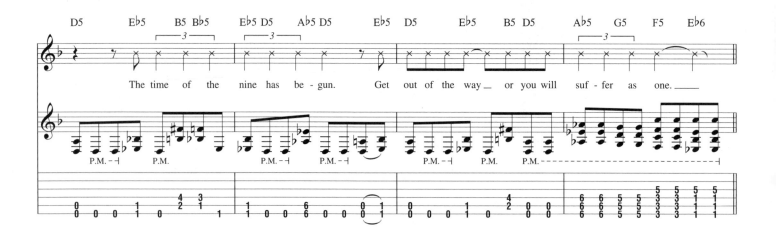

The time of the nine has be-gun. Get out of the way_ or you will suf-fer as one._____

Interlude
Double-time feel

Ah. _____

Verse
Half-time feel

2. This is so typ-i-cal, a-poc-a-lyp-tic-al. Hang-ing on a-bys-mal re-lease, Je-sus.

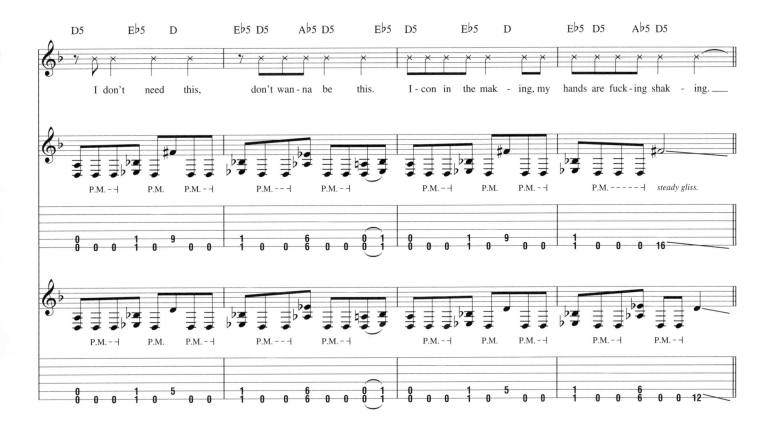

I don't need this, don't wan-na be this. I-con in the mak - ing, my hands are fuck-ing shak - ing.

Pre-Chorus
Half-time feel

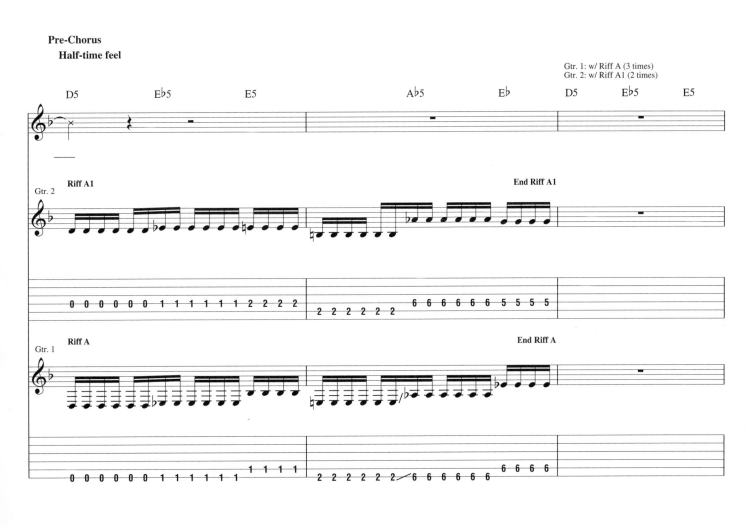

What if God does - n't care?

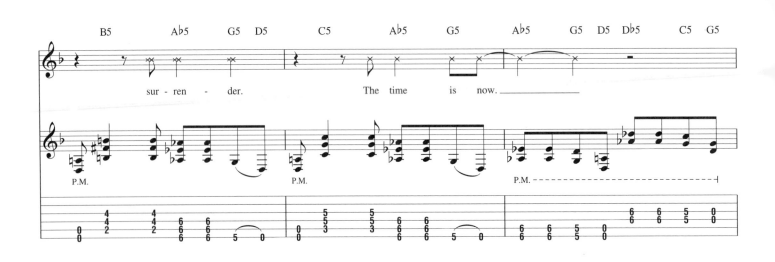

10

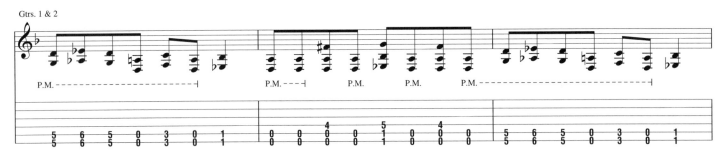

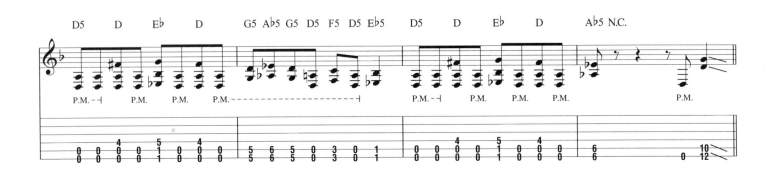

$\mathsect$ Chorus

2nd time, Gtr. 7 tacet

A - mer - i - ca is a kill - ing name. ___ It does-n't feel or dis -

crim - i - nate. ___ And life is just a kill - ing field. ___

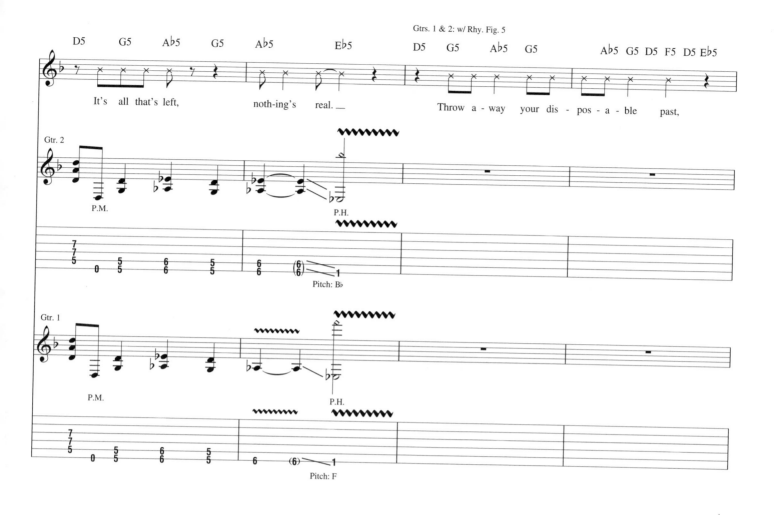

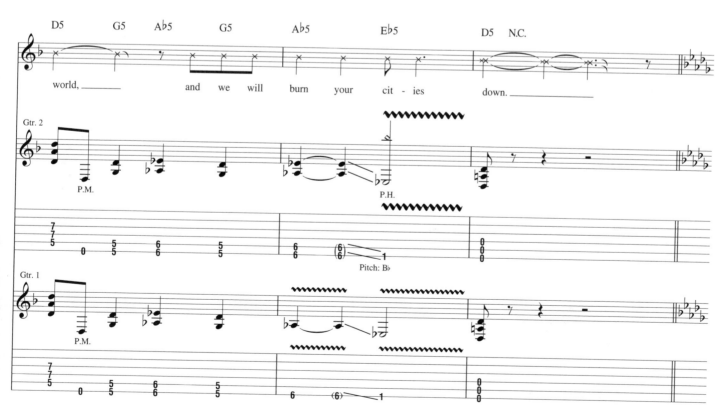

Guitar Solo

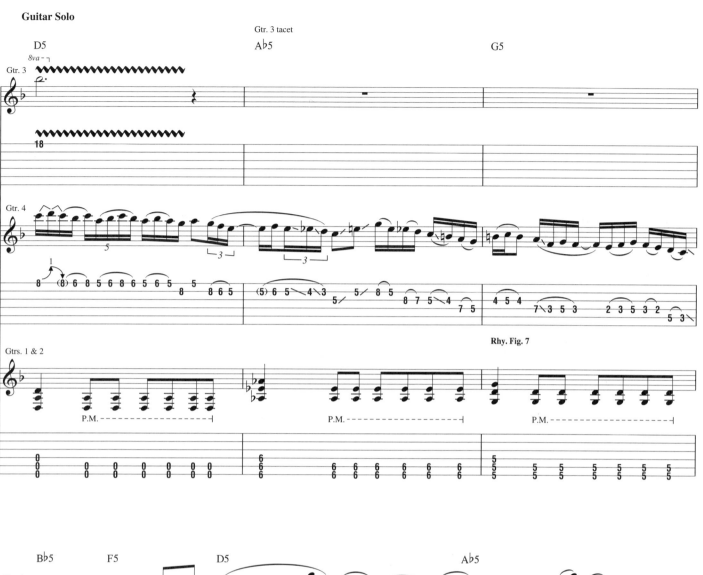

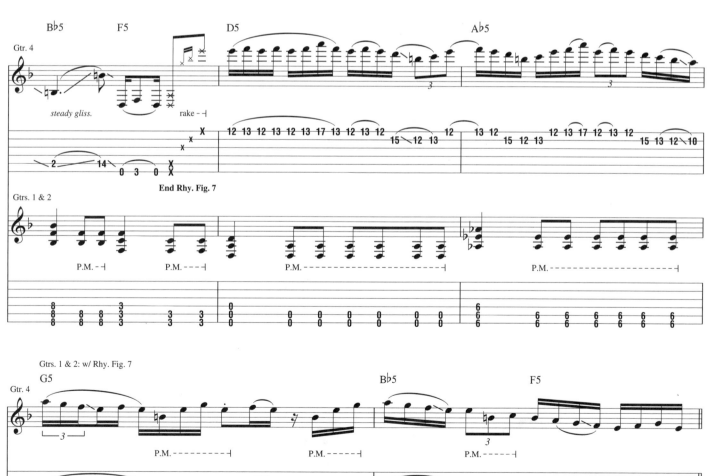

Pre-Chorus

What if God does-n't care? __

What if God does-n't care? __

Gtrs. 1 & 2: w/ Rhy. Fig. 9
Gtr. 5: w/ Riff C

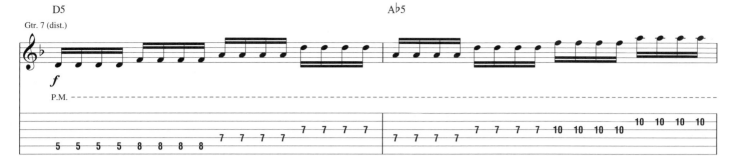

D.S. al Coda 1

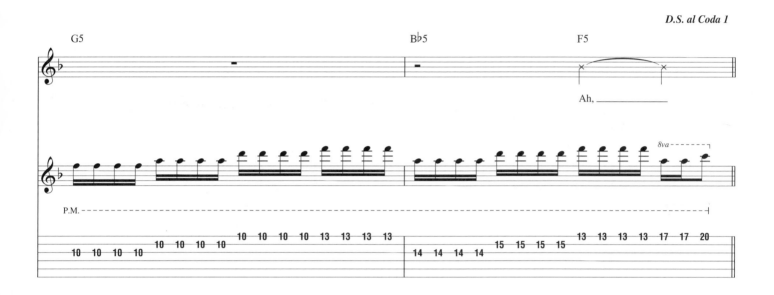

Ah, ____

Coda 1

Interlude
Slower ♩ = 144

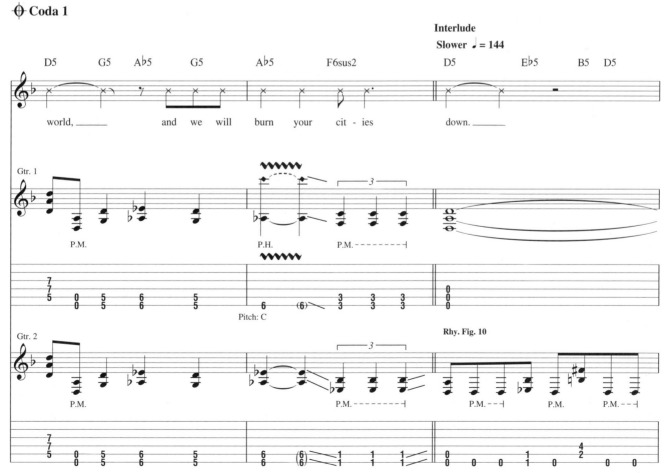

world, ____ and we will burn your cit - ies down. ____

Gtr. 1

Pitch: C

Gtr. 2

Rhy. Fig. 10

17

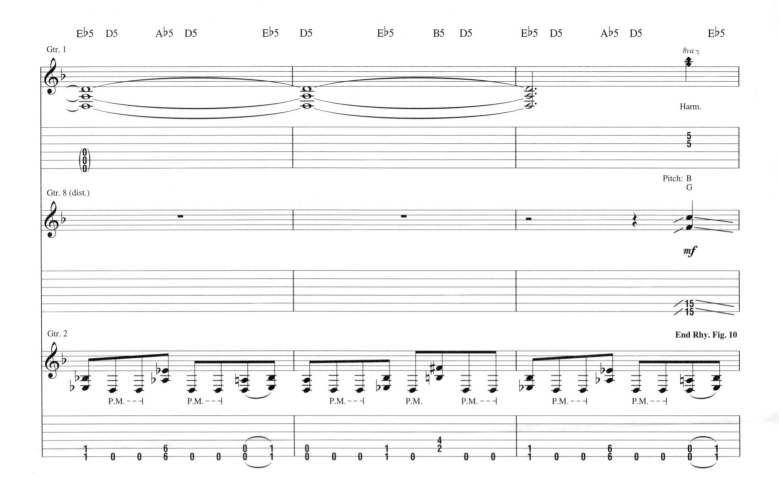

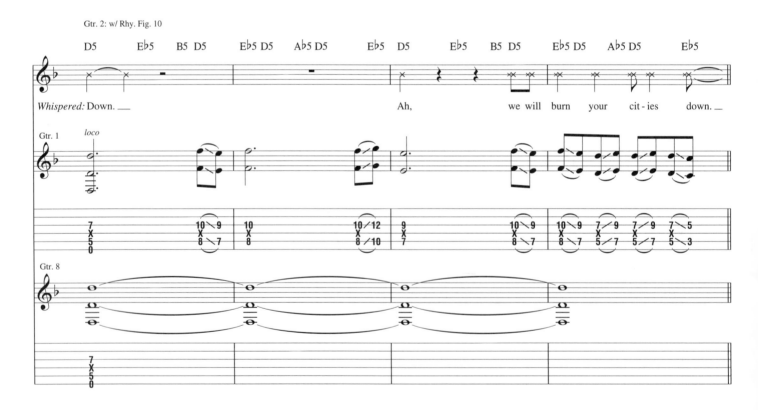

Bridge

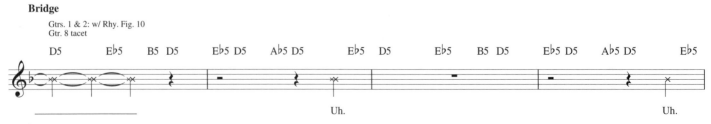

Feed them bones and pol - i - tics. ___ You wan - na rev - o - lu - tion - ize? ___

Gtr. 1: w/ Rhy. Fig. 1 (1st 6 meas.)

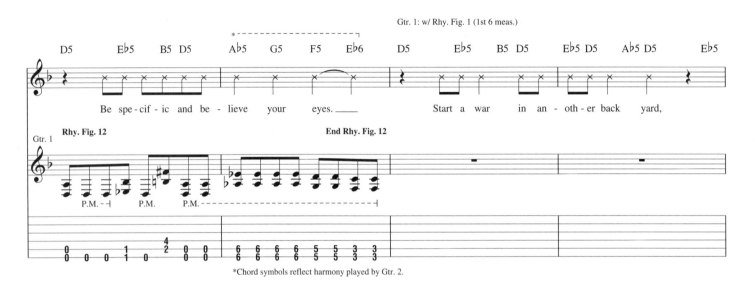

Be spe - cif - ic and be - lieve your eyes. ___ Start a war in an - oth - er back yard,

*Chord symbols reflect harmony played by Gtr. 2.

and we'll de - stroy your house of cards. ___ Give me a min - ute and I'll change your mind.

Chorus
Double-time feel

Gtr. 1: w/ Rhy. Fig. 12

Gtr. 1: w/ Rhy. Fig. 2

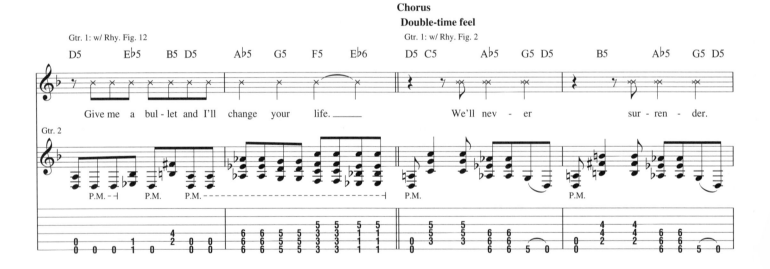

Give me a bul - let and I'll change your life. ___ We'll nev - er sur - ren - der.

Gtr. 1: w/ Rhy. Fig. 3

The time is now. ___ Con - tin - ue, we're in you, ___

Interlude

End double-time feel

Gtr. 1: w/ Rhy. Fig. 4

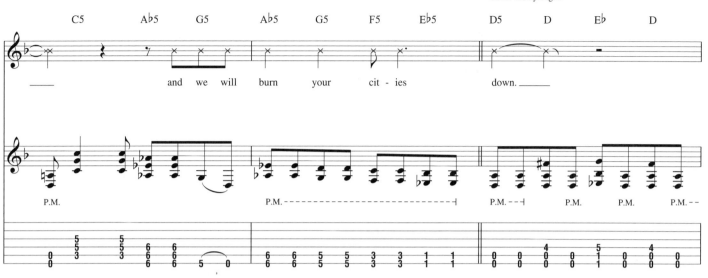

and we will burn your cit - ies down.

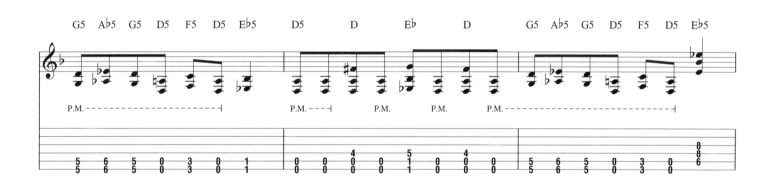

D.S. al Coda 2

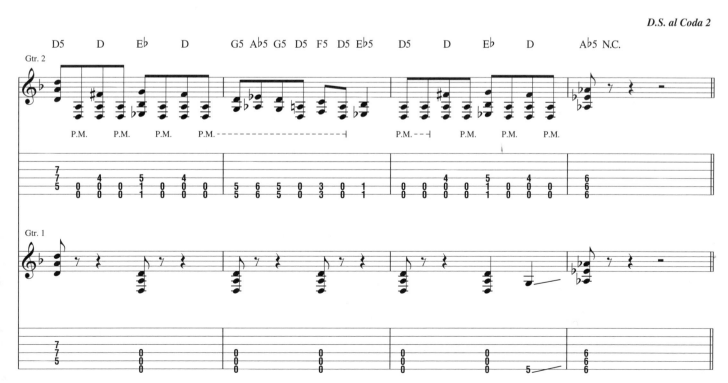

Coda 2

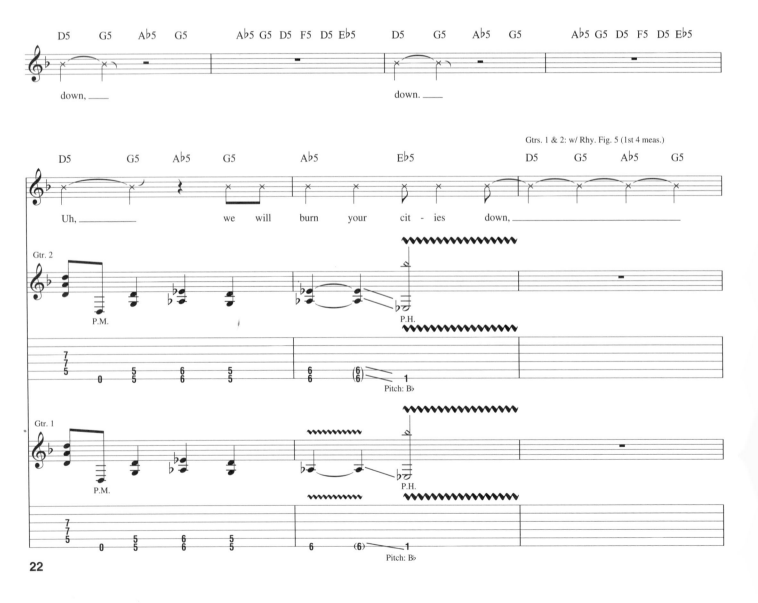

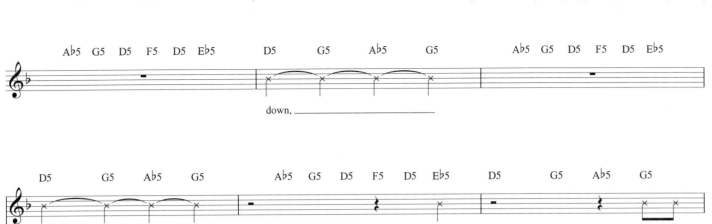

down, _____

down. _____   Huh,   we will

Gtrs. 1 & 2

P.M.   P.M. - - - - - - - - - - - - -   P.M.

Outro
Slower ♩ = 136

Gtrs. 1 & 2: w/ Rhy. Fig. 10

burn   your   cit-ies   down. _____

Gtr. 2

Gtr. 9 (slight dist.)

P.M. - - - - - - - - - -

mf
w/ rotary wah

Gtr. 1

P.H.   P.M. - - - - - - - - - -

Pitch: F

Gtrs. 1 & 2: w/ Rhy. Fig. 11

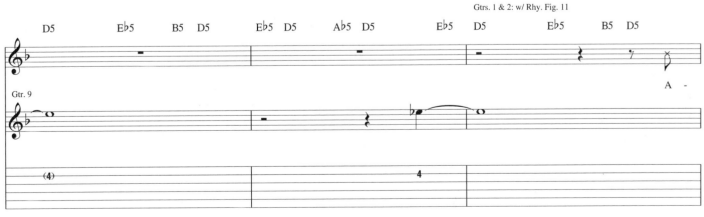

Gtr. 9

A -

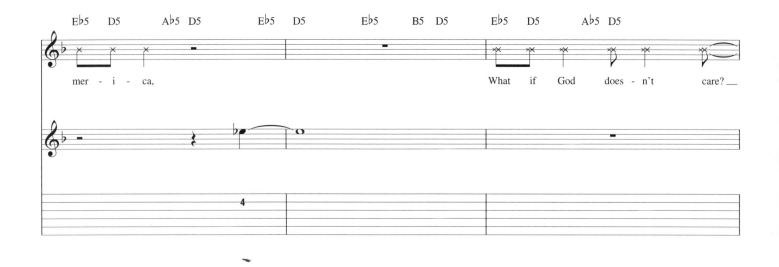

Gtr. 9: w/ Riff D (3 times)

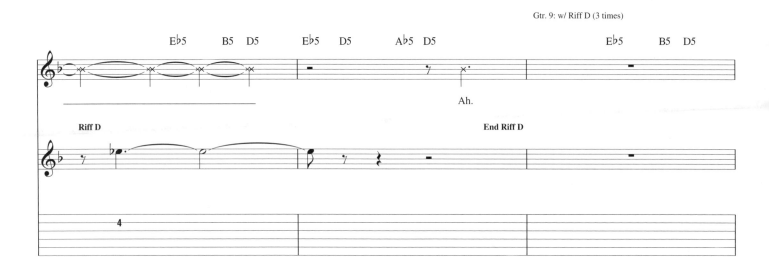

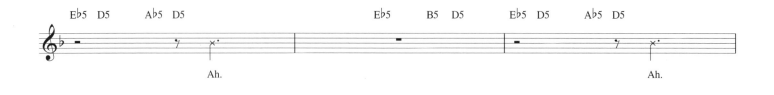

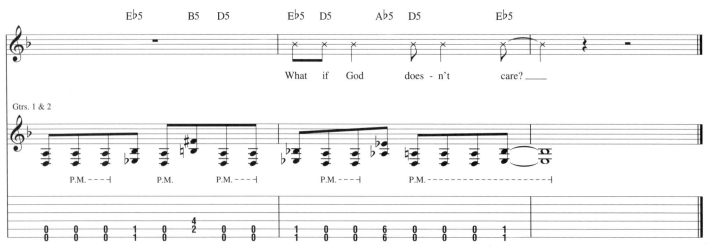

Sulfur
Words and Music by Slipknot

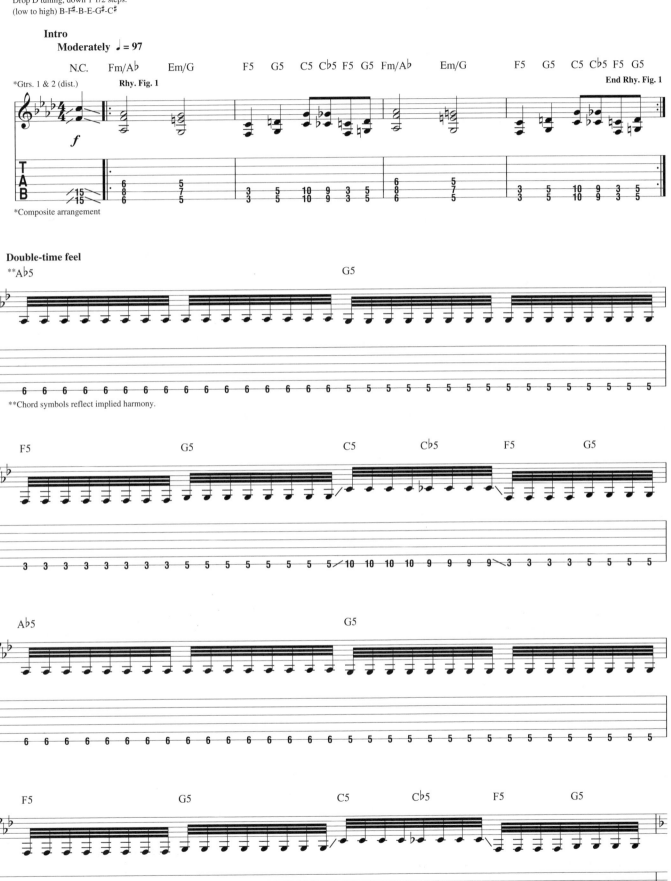

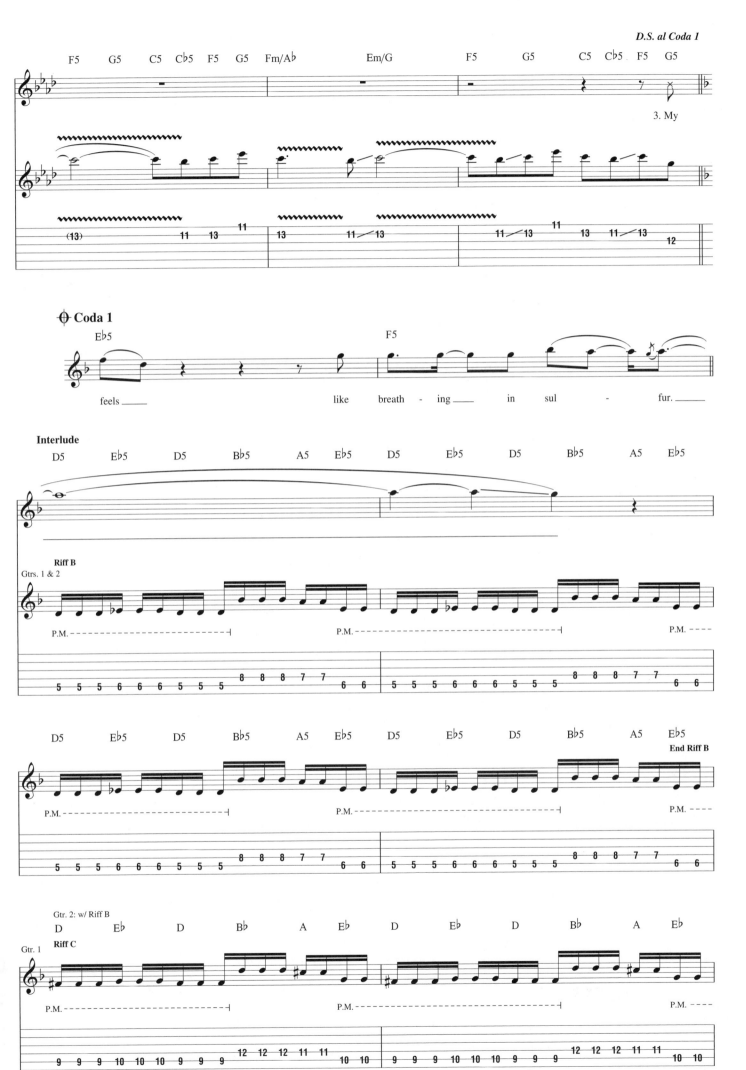

29

Psychosocial

Words and Music by Slipknot

Drop D tuning, down 2 1/2 steps:
(low to high) A-E-A-D-F#-B

Intro

Moderately fast ♩ = 135

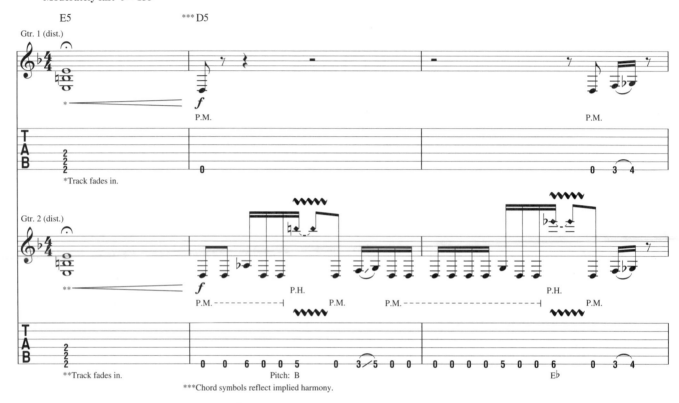

*Track fades in.

**Track fades in.

***Chord symbols reflect implied harmony.

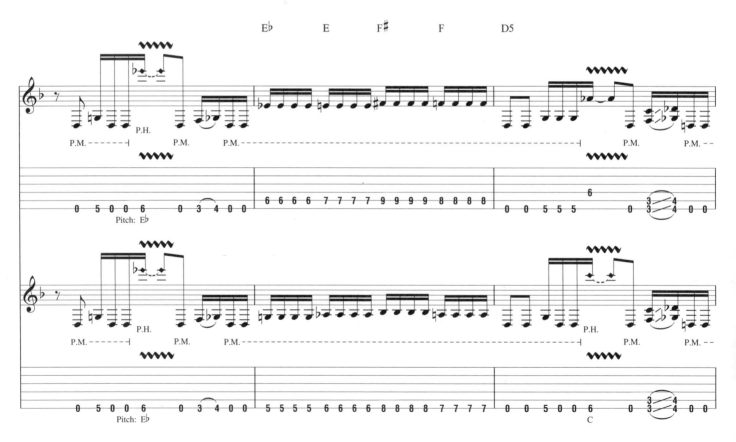

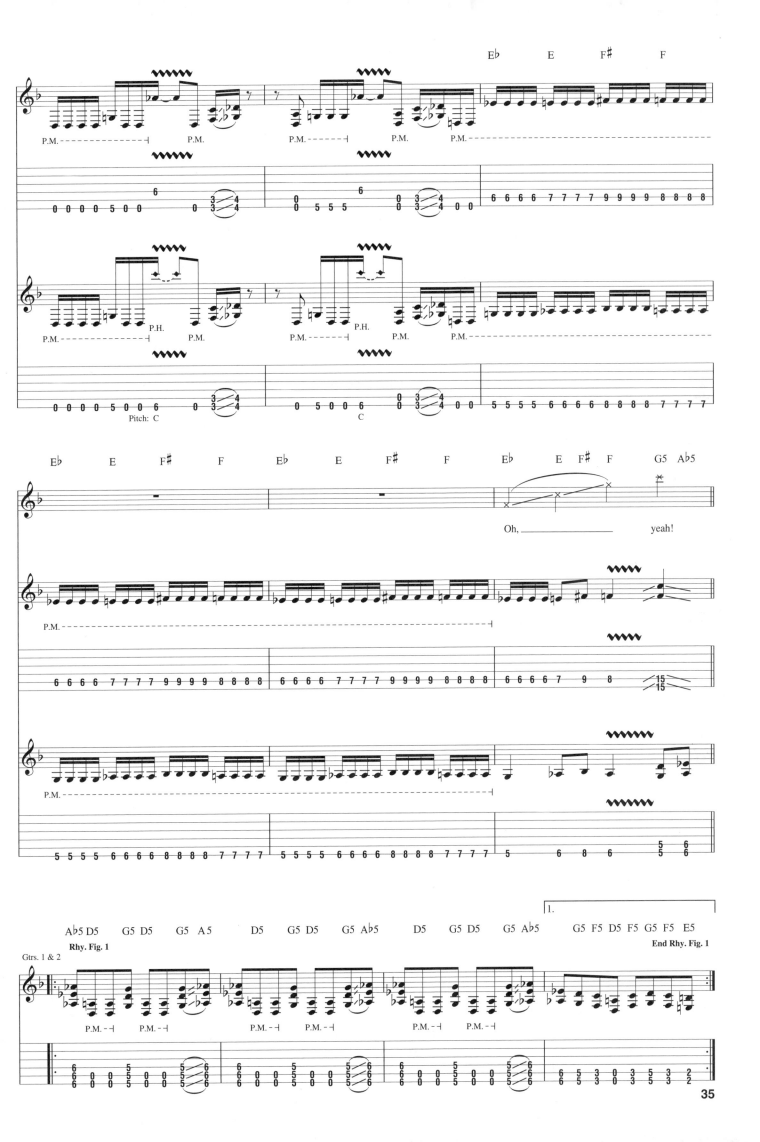

Guitar Solo

Gtrs. 1 & 2: w/ Rhy. Fig. 1 (1st 2 meas., 4 times)
Gtr. 3 tacet

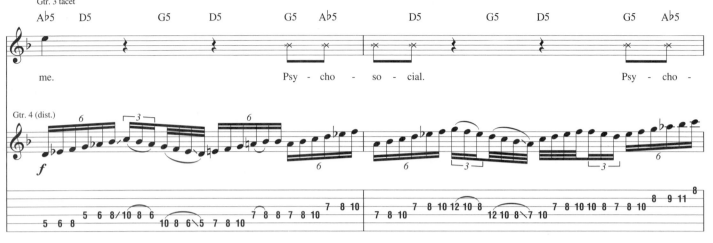

Gtr. 4 (dist.)

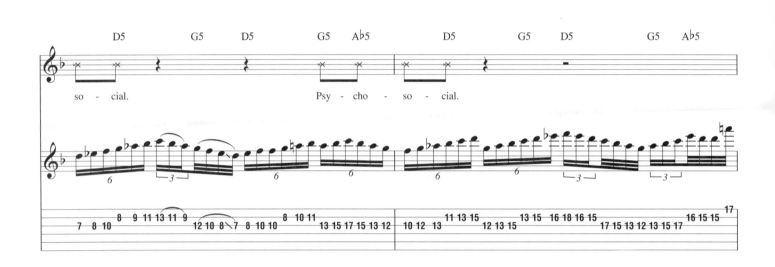

Voc. Fig. 1   End Voc. Fig. 1

Gtr. 5 (dist.)

Gtr. 4

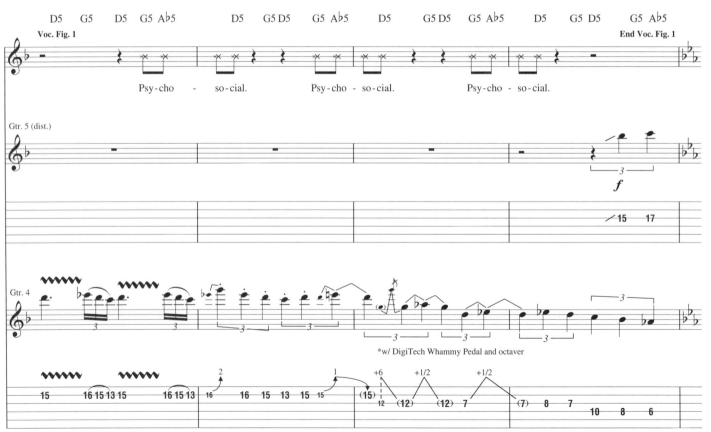

*w/ DigiTech Whammy Pedal and octaver

*Set Whammy Pedal for one octave above when depressed (toe down).
Set octaver for one octave above.

Dead Memories

Words and Music by Slipknot

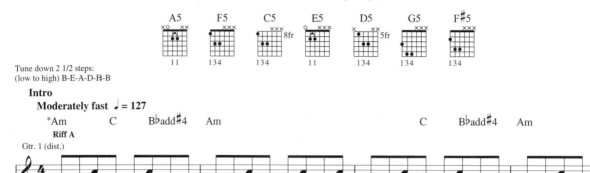

Tune down 2 1/2 steps:
(low to high) B-E-A-D-F♯-B

Intro
Moderately fast ♩ = 127

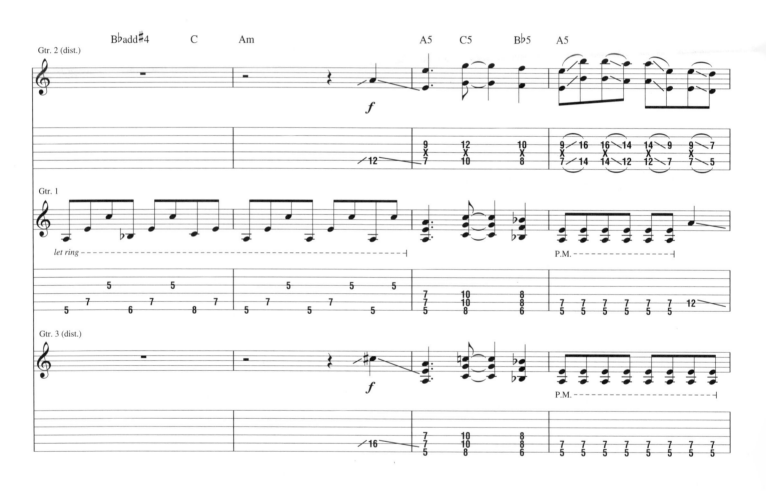

*Chord symbols reflect implied harmony.

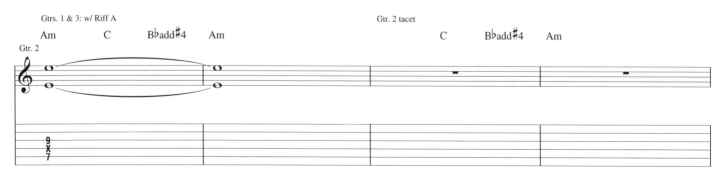

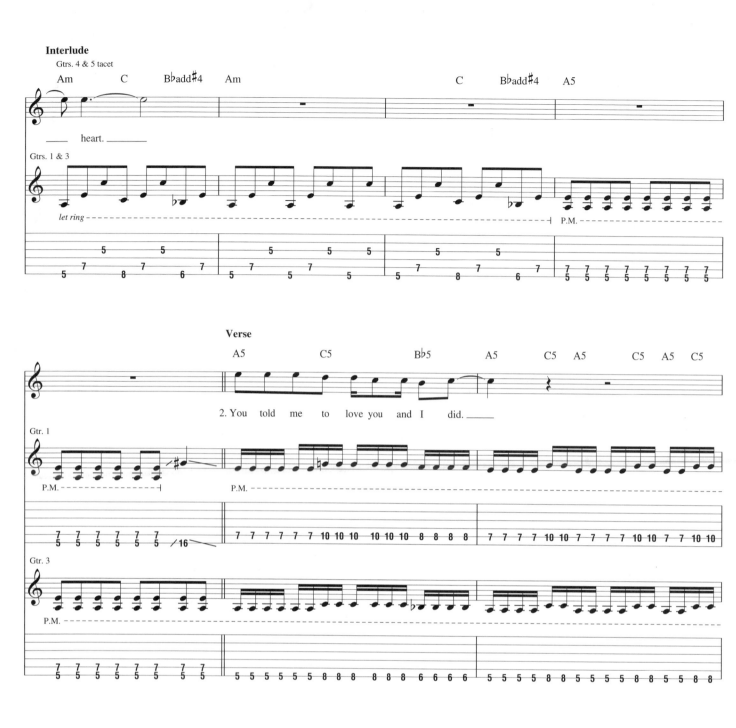

48

Vendetta

Words and Music by Slipknot

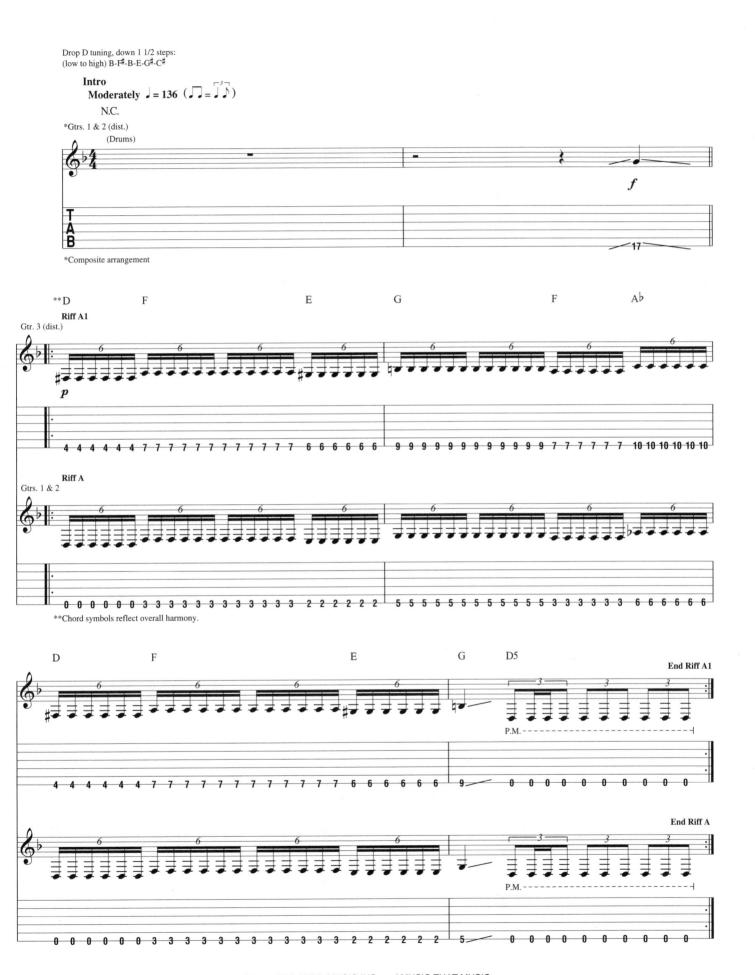

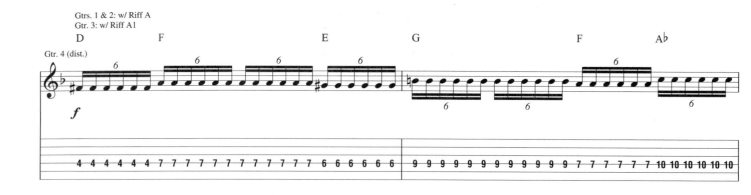

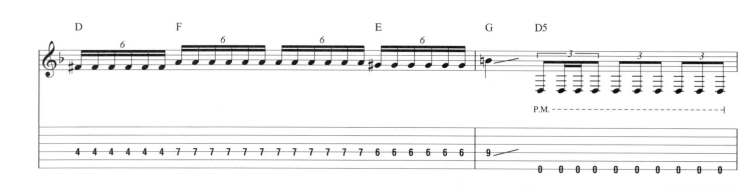

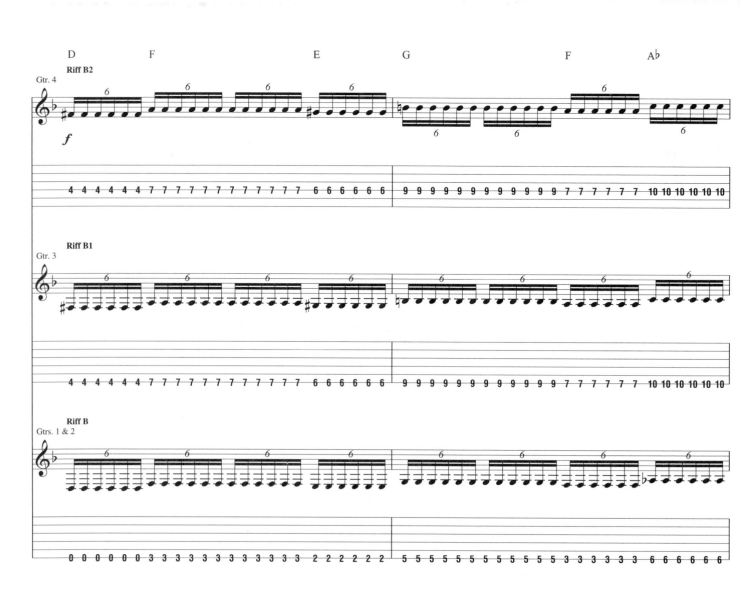

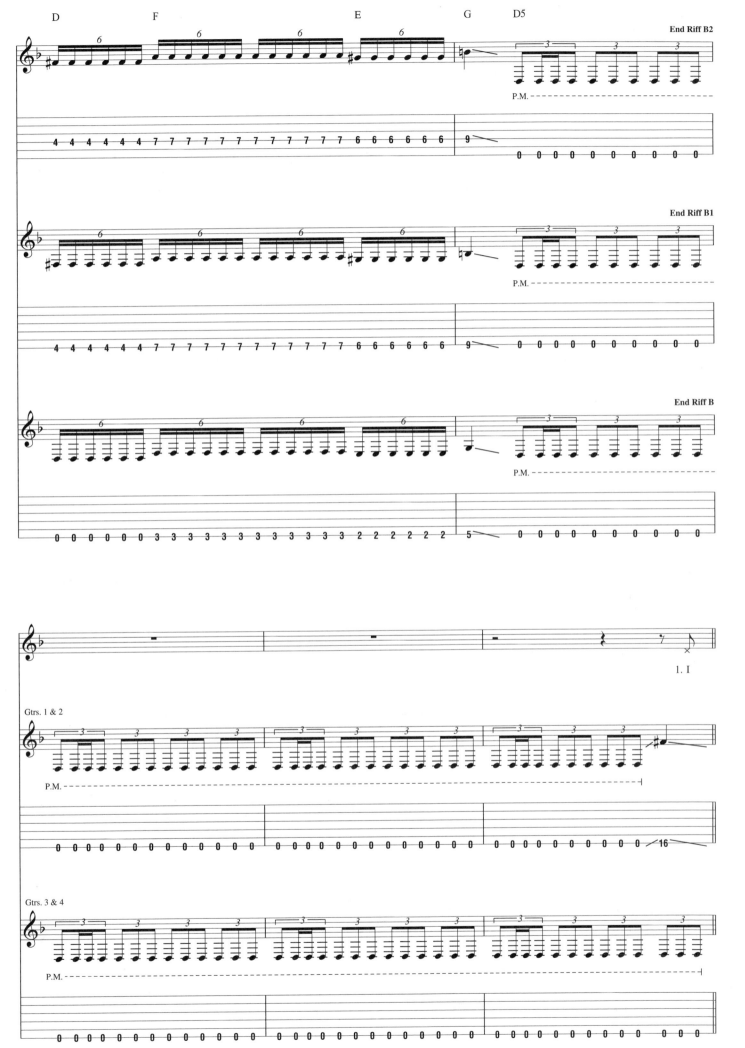

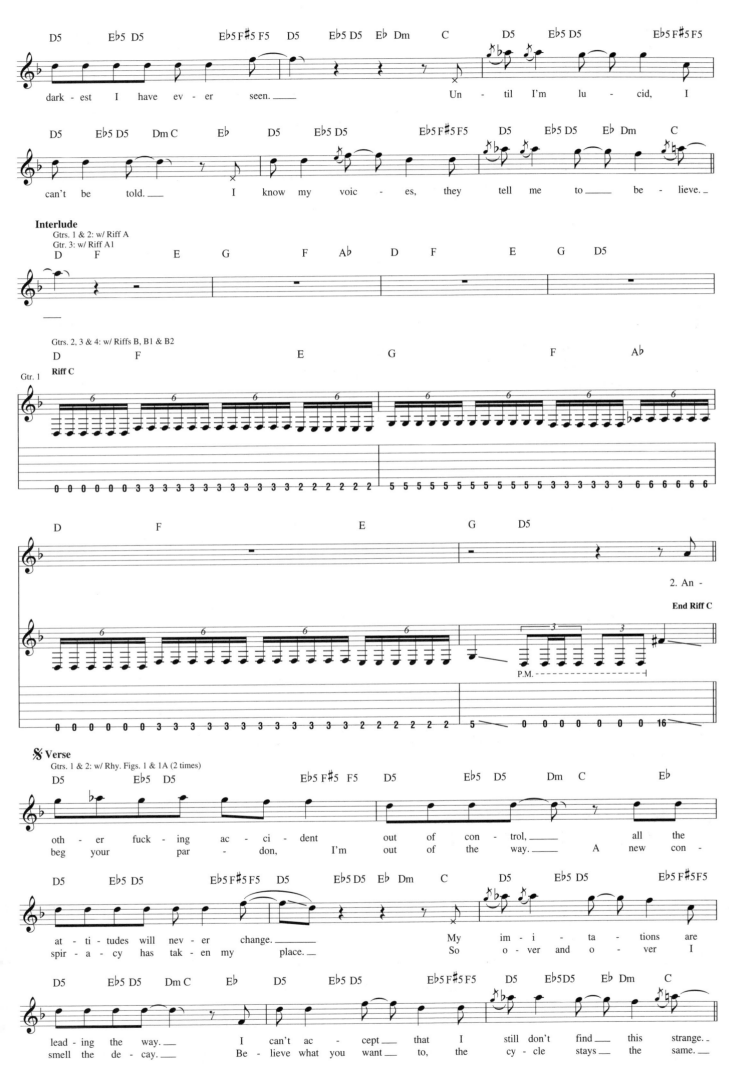

Chorus
D5 Ab5 G5 D5 F5 D5 Bb5 A5 D5 Eb5 D5 Ab5 G5 D5 F5 D5 F5 E5 Eb5
*Voc. Fig. 1
End Voc. Fig. 1
Are you ready - y for the time of your
(Hey, hey. Hey, hey. Hey, hey.)
Riff D
Gtr. 5 (dist.)
End Riff D
mf
Riff E
Gtr. 6 (dist.)
mf
Riff E1
Gtr. 7 (dist.)
mf
Rhy. Fig. 3
Gtrs. 1 & 2
End Rhy. Fig. 3
P.M. P.M. P.M. P.M. P.M. P.M. P.M.
*Refers to downstemmed voc. only.
To Coda 1
Bkgd. Voc.: w/ Voc. Fig. 1
Gtrs. 1 & 2: w/ Rhy. Fig. 3
Gtr. 5: w/ Riff D
D5 Ab5 G5 D5 F5 D5 Bb5 A5 D5 Eb5 D5 Ab5 G5 D5 F5 D5 F5 E5 Eb5
life? Are you ready - y for the time of your life?
Gtr. 6
End Riff E
Gtr. 7
End Riff E1

Butcher's Hook

Words and Music by Slipknot

Drop D tuning, down 1 1/2 steps:
(low to high) B-F#-B-E-G#-C#

*Gtr. 3 (dist.) played **f**, w/ wah-wah.
**Chord symbols reflect overall harmony.

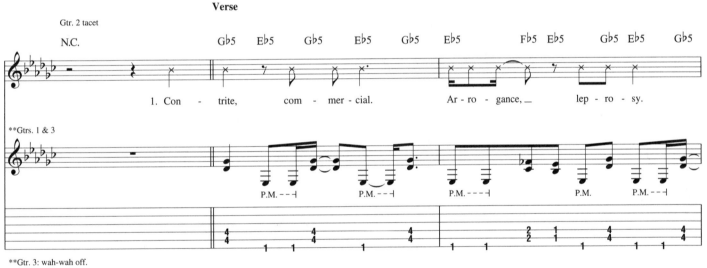

**Gtr. 3: wah-wah off.

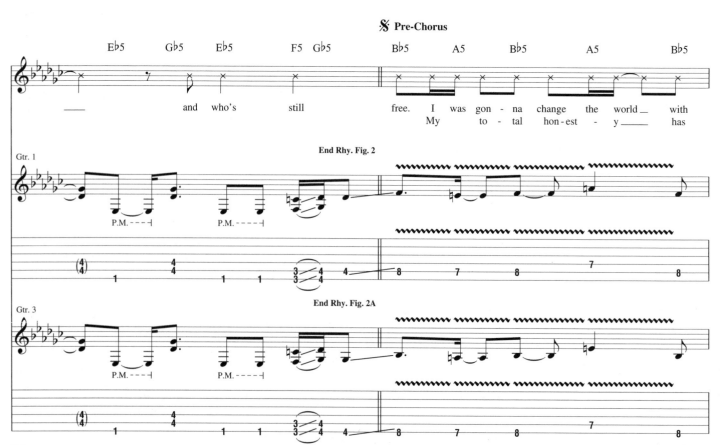

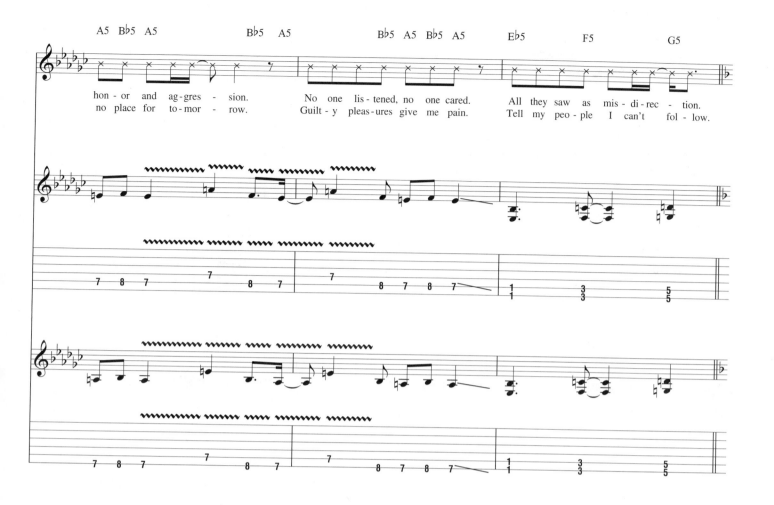

honor and aggression.
no place for tomorrow.

No one listened, no one cared.
Guilty pleasures give me pain.

All they saw as misdirection.
Tell my people I can't follow.

Chorus

Go ahead and disagree.

I'm giving up again.

Go ahead and disagree.

Rhy. Fig. 3

Rhy. Fig. 3A

Outro

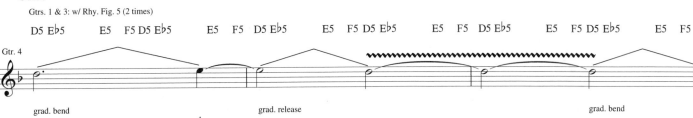

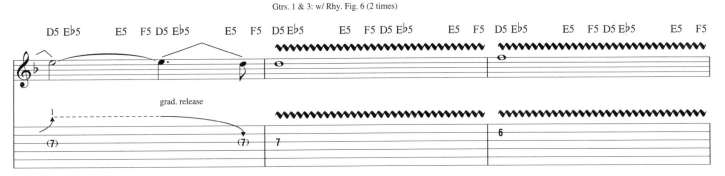

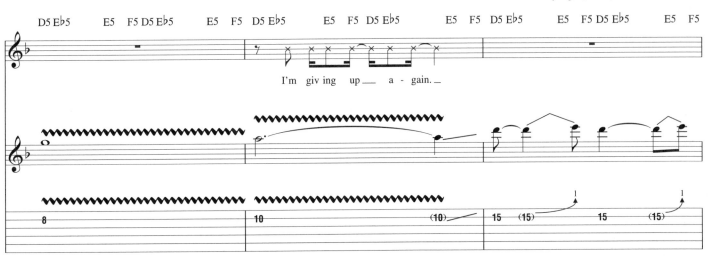

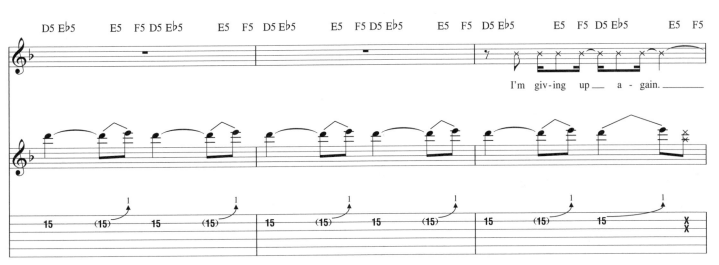

Gehenna

Words and Music by Slipknot

Drop D tuning, down 2 1/2 steps:
(low to high) A-E-A-D-F♯-B

Intro
Moderately ♩ = 100

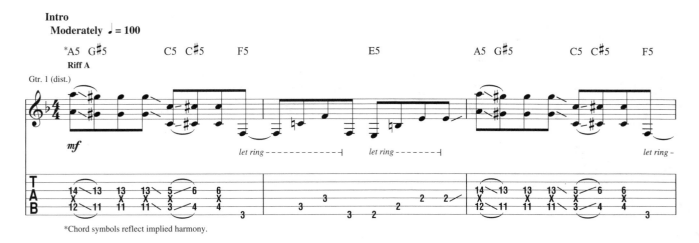

*Chord symbols reflect implied harmony.

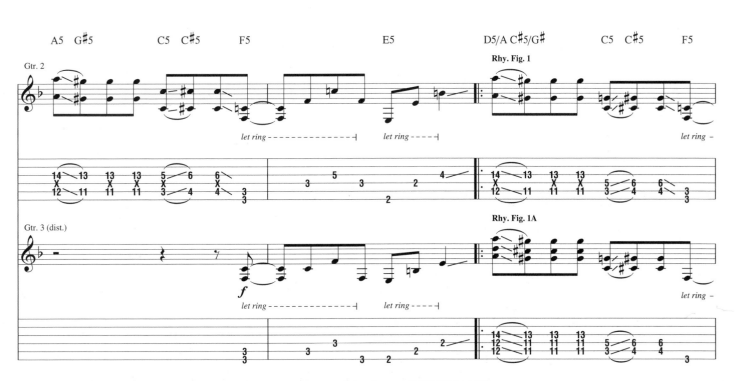

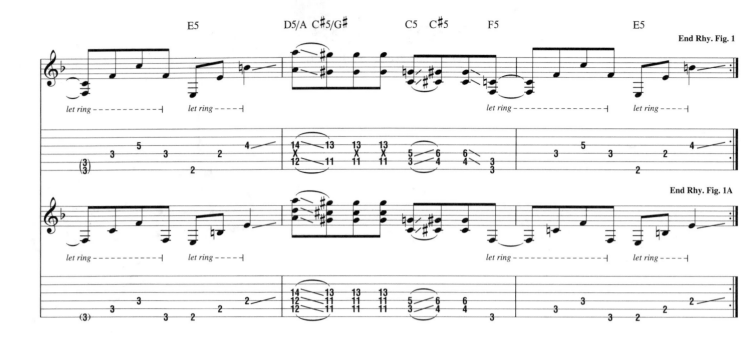

Verse

Gtr. 2 tacet

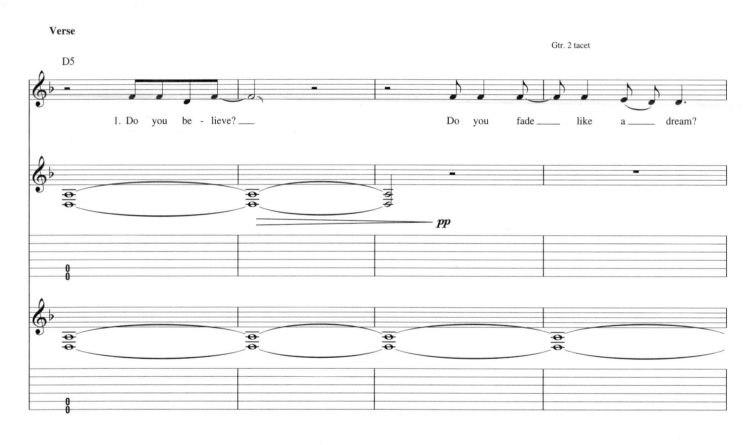

1. Do you be - lieve? ____ Do you fade ____ like a ____ dream?

Let me hear ____ you breathe. ____ Let me watch ____ as you ____ sleep.

Gtr. 3

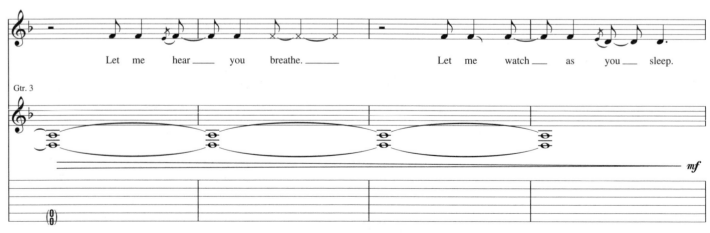

Verse

2. The blood and the bod - y ___ con - trol the cut ___ so it's seam - less.

Show me your heart. ___ Show me the way ___ to com - plete ___ this.

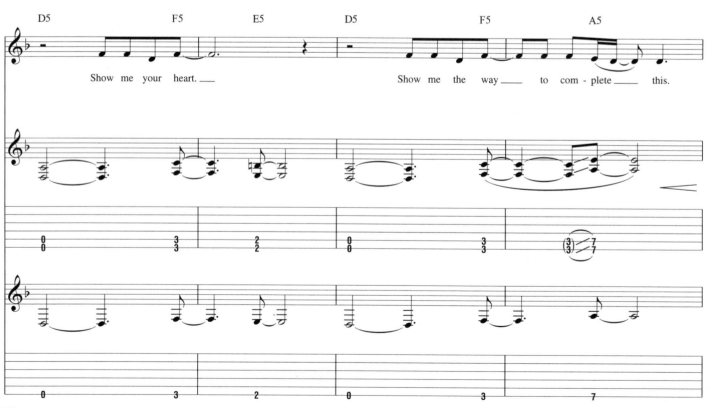

Interlude

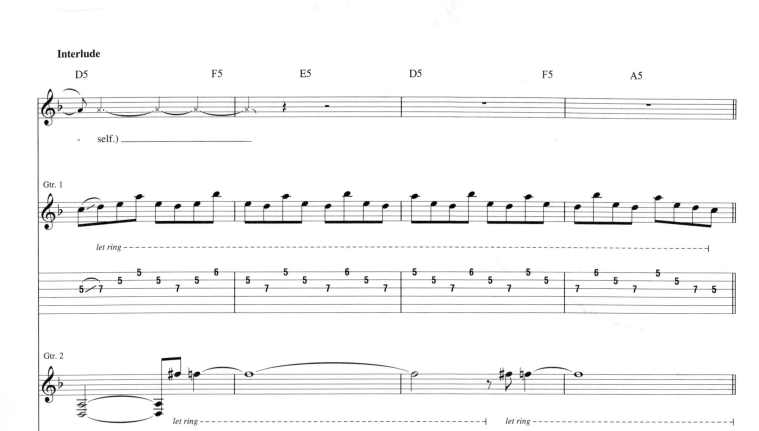

Guitar Solo

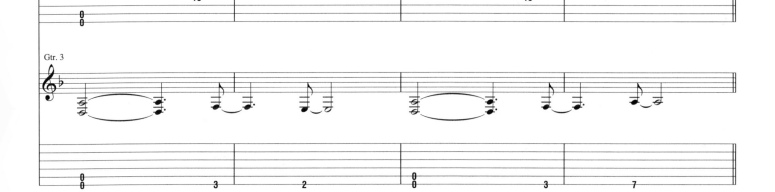

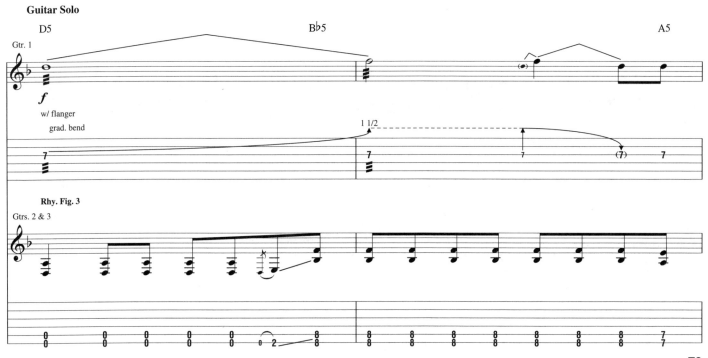

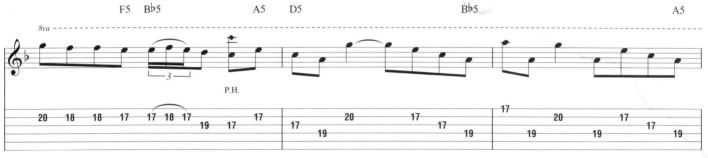

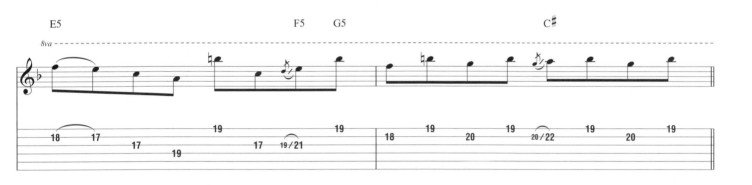

Verse

Gtr. 2: w/ Riff B

Gtr. 1 tacet

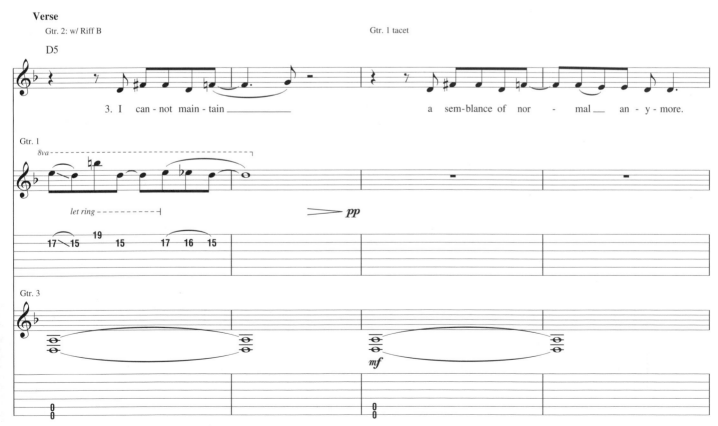

3. I can - not main - tain _____ a sem - blance of nor - mal _____ an - y - more.

Outro

Gtr. 2: w/ Riff B (1st 6 meas.)

D5

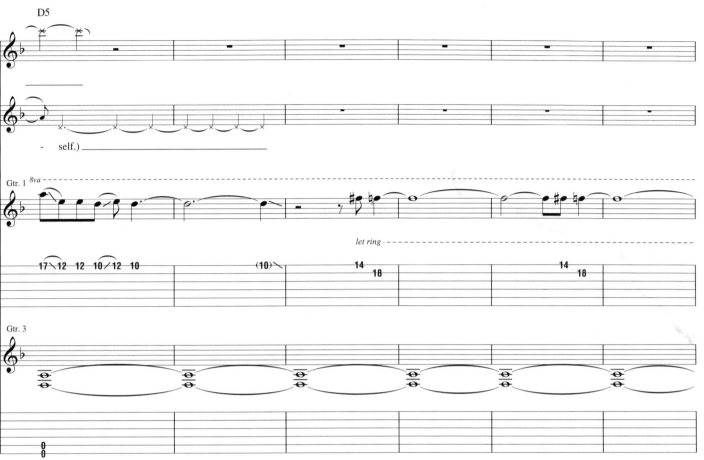

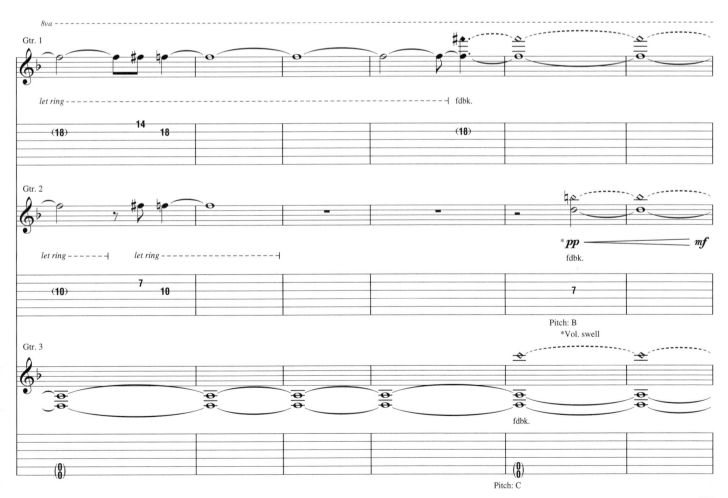

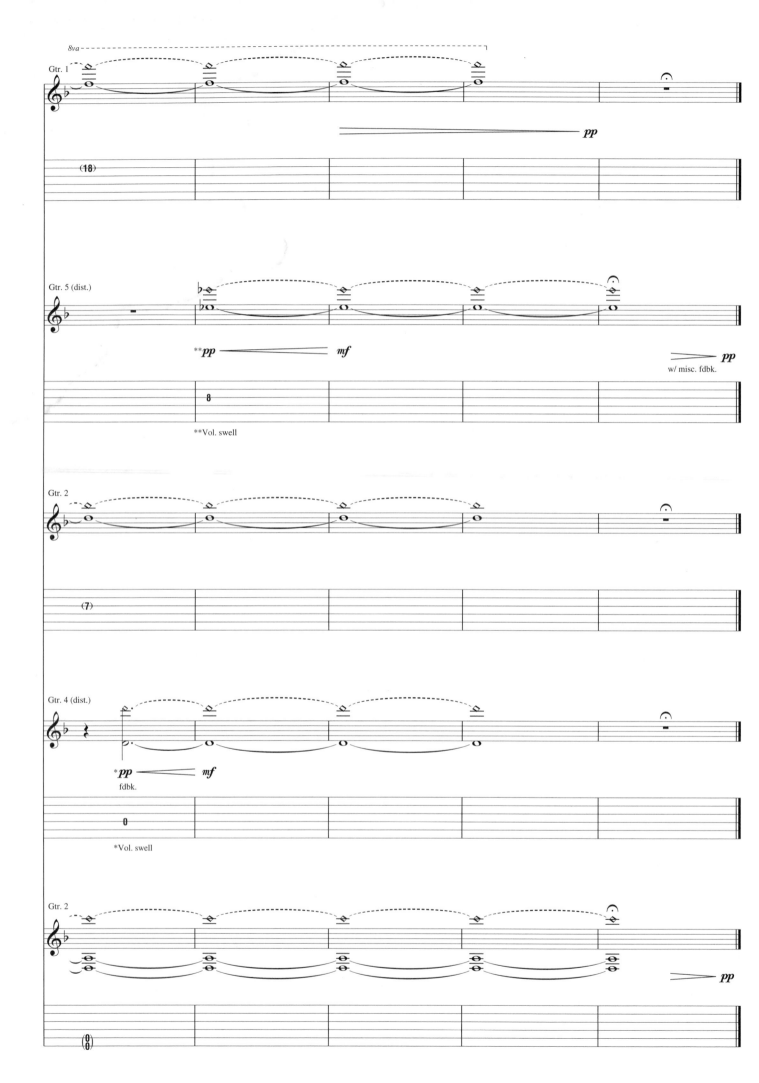

This Cold Black

Words and Music by Slipknot

Drop D tuning, down 2 1/2 steps:
(low to high) A-E-A-D-F#-B

Intro
Fast ♩ = 210

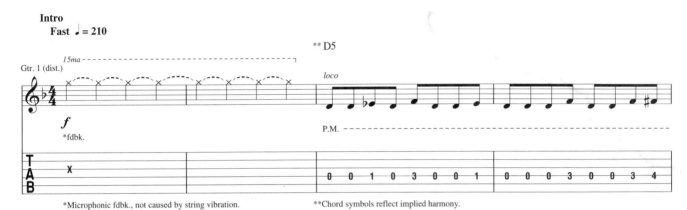

*Microphonic fdbk., not caused by string vibration.
**Chord symbols reflect implied harmony.

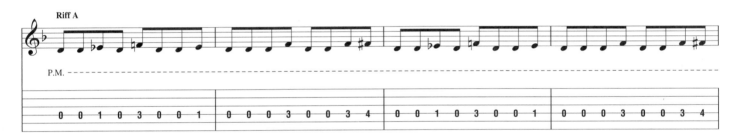

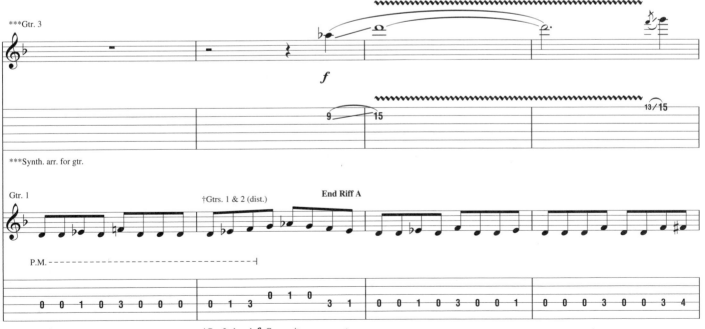

*†Gtr. 2 played **f**. Composite arrangement*

Bridge
Half-time feel

You ut - ter waste of tired ___ flesh, it does-n't mat - ter if you can't pro - gress.

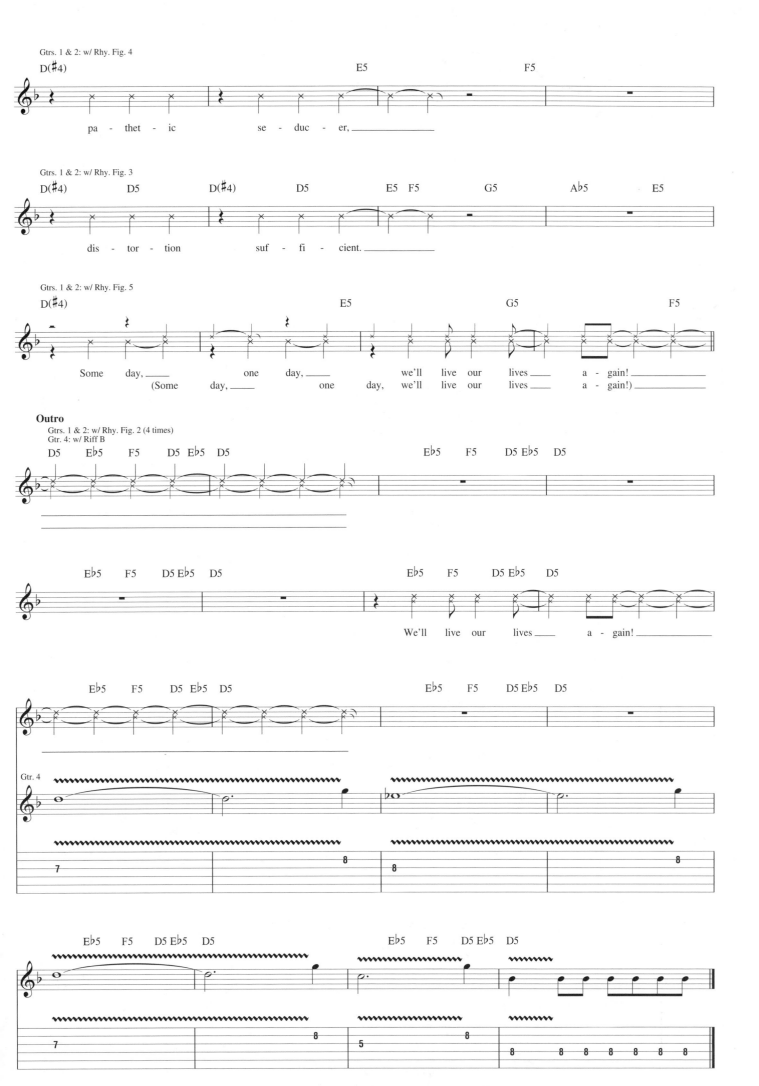

Wherein Lies Continue

Words and Music by Slipknot

Drop D tuning, down 2 1/2 steps:
(low to high) A-E-A-D-F♯-B

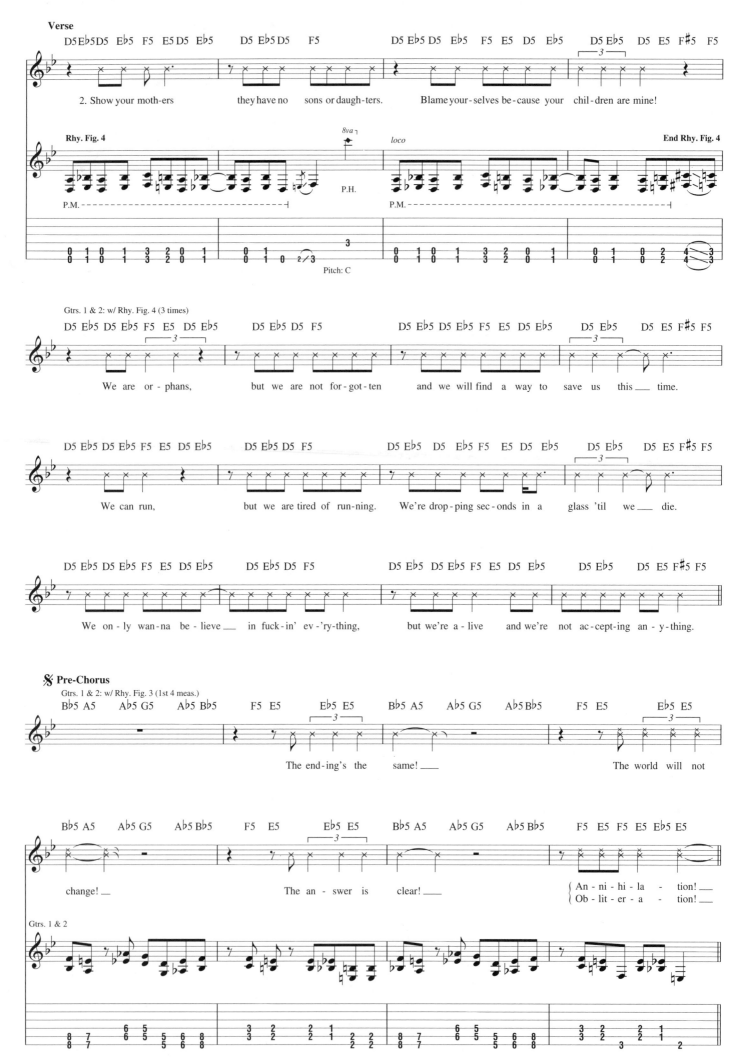

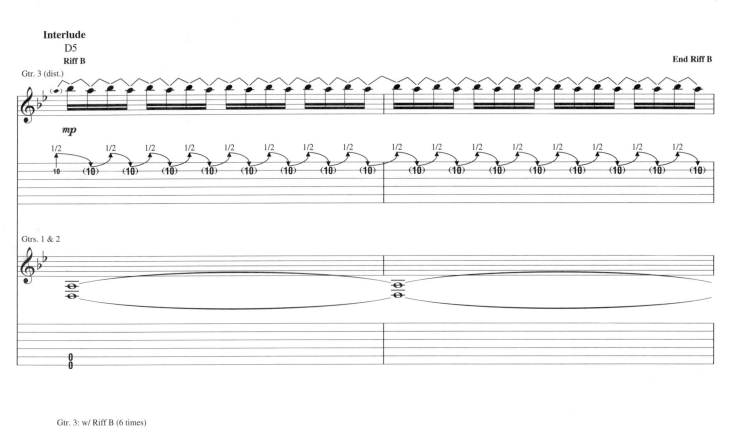

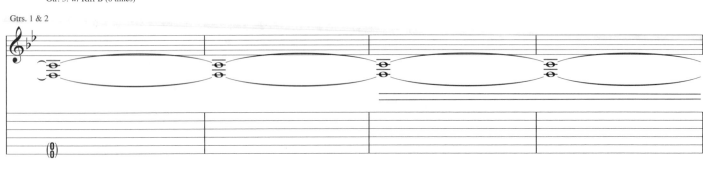

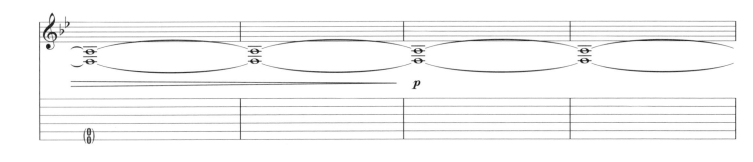

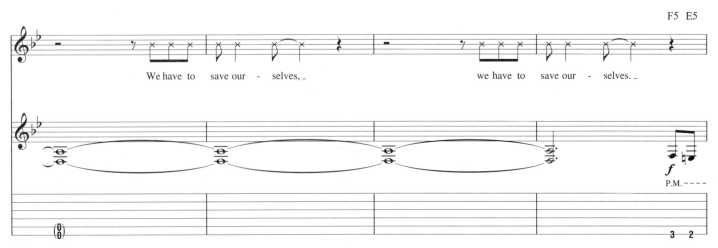

Verse
F♯5 G5 F♯5 G5 A♭5 G5 F♯5 G5 F♯5 G5 F♯5 A♭5 A5 F♯5 G5 F♯5 G5 A♭5 G5 F♯5 G5 F♯5 G5 F♯5 G5
kill your fath-ers, de-stroy an-oth-er life. Ques-tion ev-'ry-thing we clung to for years.
Rhy. Fig. 2
End Rhy. Fig. 2
P.M.
Gtrs. 1 & 2: w/ Rhy. Fig. 2 (3 times)
F♯5 G5 F♯5 G5 A♭5 G5 F♯5 G5 F♯5 G5 F♯5 A♭5 A5 F♯5 G5 F♯5 G5 A♭5 G5 F♯5 G5 F♯5 G5 F♯5 G5
Live for-ev-er, de-sign a bet-ter death. Con-fuse a li-ar with a sav-ior from fear.
F♯5 G5 F♯5 G5 A♭5 G5 F♯5 G5 F♯5 G5 F♯5 A♭5 A5 F♯5 G5 F♯5 G5 A♭5 G5 F♯5 G5 F♯5 G5 F♯5 G5
Cre-ate a myth, and sep-a-rate the cho-sen ones. Ad-o-les-cent in-de-pend-ence, do-min-ion.
F♯5 G5 F♯5 G5 A♭5 G5 F♯5 G5 F♯5 G5 F♯5 A♭5 A5 F♯5 G5 F♯5 G5 A♭5 G5 F♯5 G5 F♯5 G5 F♯5 G5
I on-ly wan-na be-lieve in fuck-in' an-y-thing, but now my con-science is con-tra-dict-ing ev-'ry-thing!
Pre-Chorus
B♭5 A5 A♭5 G5 A♭5 B♭5 F5 E5 E♭5 E5 B♭5 A5 A♭5 G5 A♭5 B♭5 F5 E5 E♭5 E5
The end-ing's the same! The world will not
Rhy. Fig. 3
Gtrs. 1 & 2
End Rhy. Fig. 3
B♭5 A5 A♭5 G5 A♭5 B♭5 F5 E5 E♭5 E5 B♭5 A5 A♭5 G5 A♭5 B♭5 F5 E5 F5 E5 E♭5 E5
change! The an-swer is clear!

We have to save our - selves, _ we have to save our - selves. _

Snuff

Words and Music by Slipknot

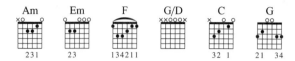

Tune down 1 1/2 steps:
(low to high) C#-F#-B-E-G#-C#

Intro
Slowly ♩ = 62

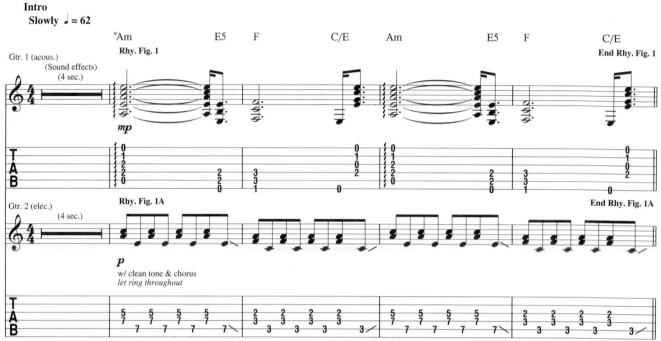

*Chord symbols reflect overall harmony.

Verse

Gtrs. 1 & 2: w/ Rhy. Figs. 1 & 1A (2 times)

1. Bur - y all ___ your se - crets in ___ my skin. ___ Come a - way ___ with in - no - cence ___ and

leave me with ___ my sins. ___ The air a - round ___ me still ___ feels like ___ a cage, ___ and

love is just ___ a cam - ou - flage ___ for what re - sem - bles rage ___ a - gain.

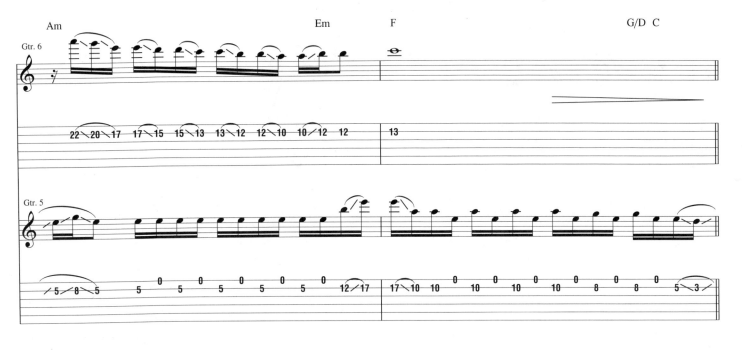

Verse

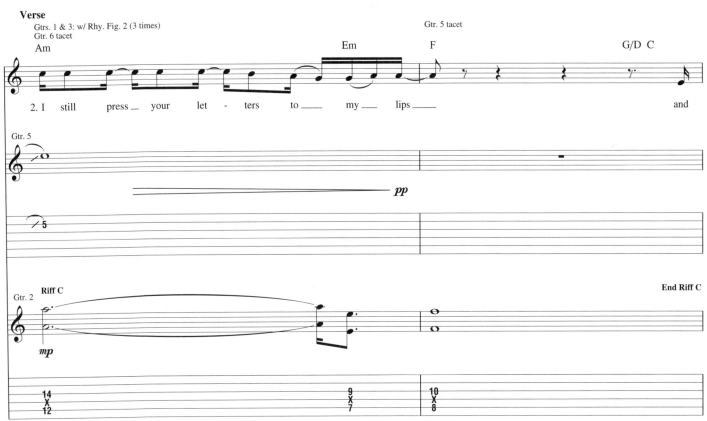

2. I still press your let - ters to my lips and

cher - ish them in parts of me that sa - vor ev - 'ry kiss. I

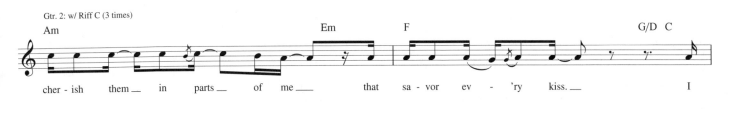

could - n't face a life with - out your light, but

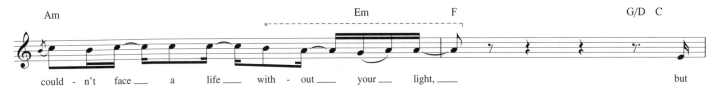

*w/ echo set for half-note regeneration w/ 1 repeat.

Gtrs. 1 & 3: w/ Rhy. Fig. 3

So break your-self a-gainst_ my_

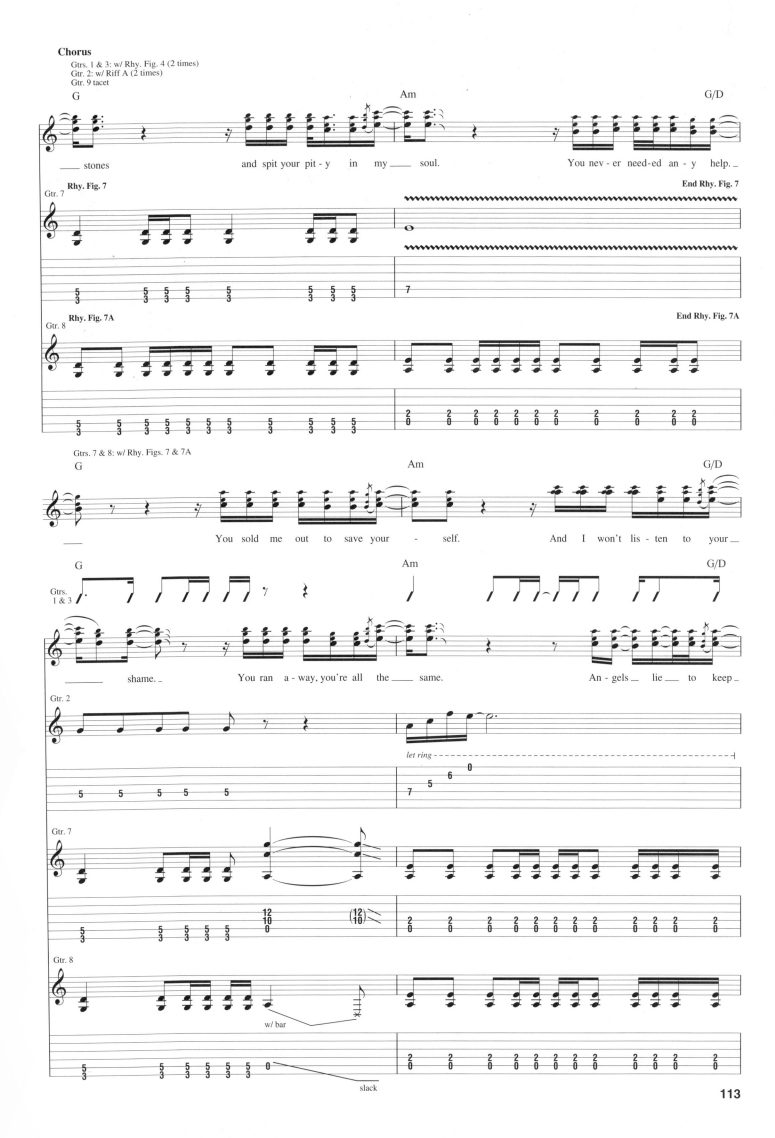

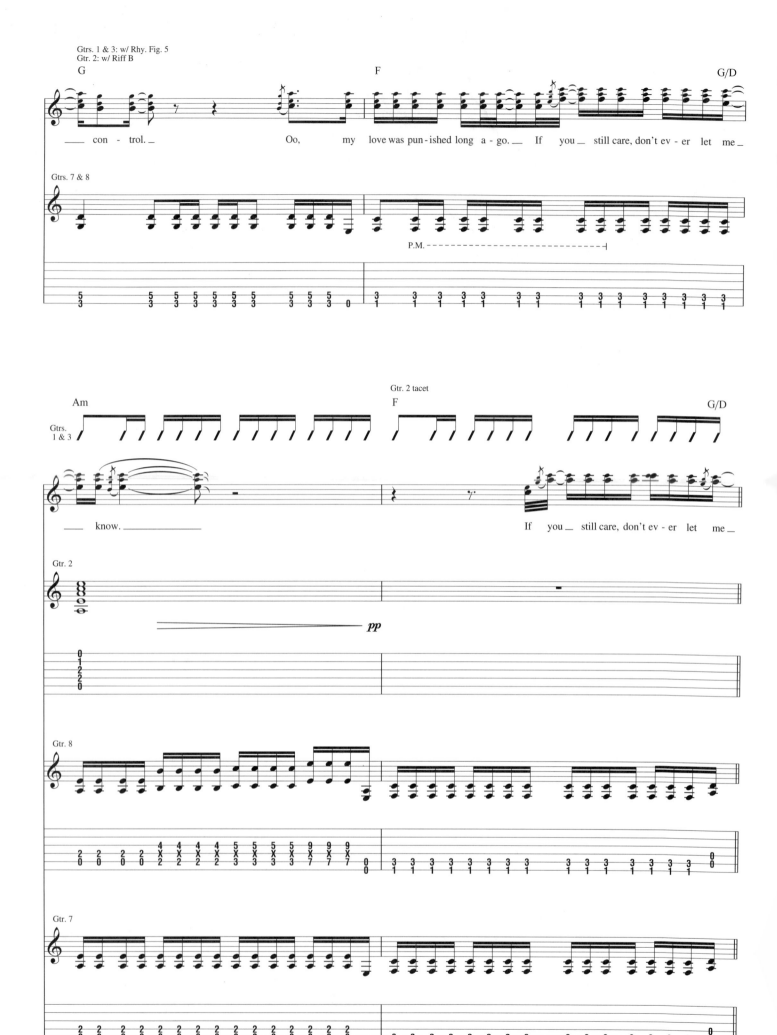

Outro

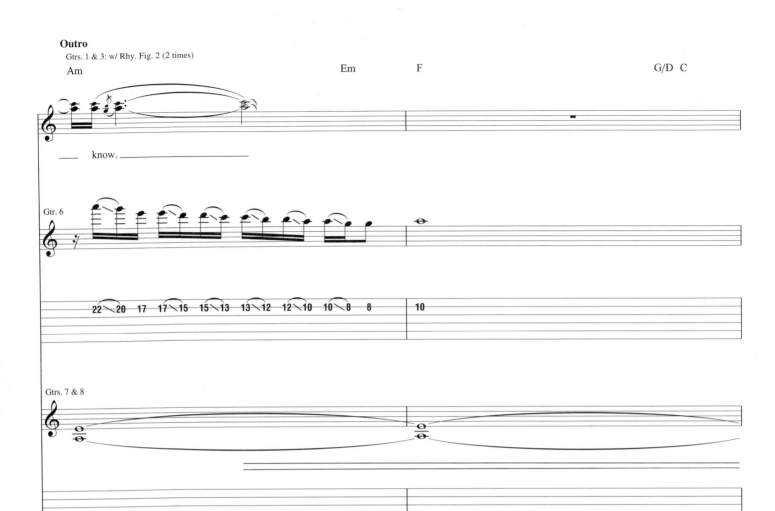

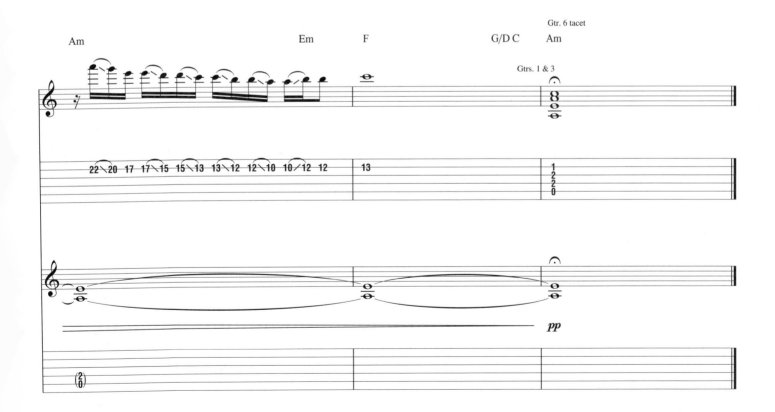

All Hope Is Gone
Words and Music by Slipknot

Drop D tuning, down 1 1/2 steps:
(low to high) B-F#-B-E-G#-C#

Intro
Fast ♩ = 200

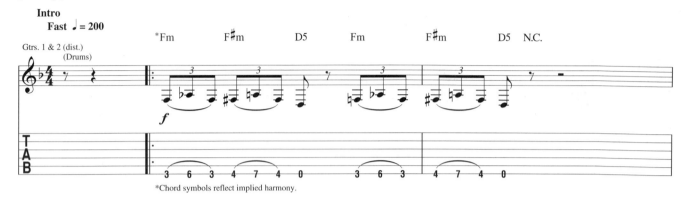

*Chord symbols reflect implied harmony.

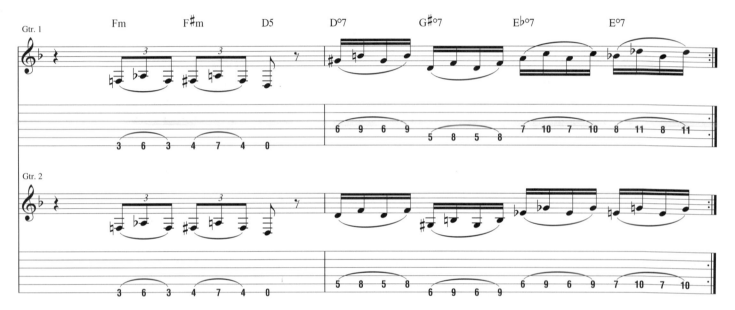

**Composite arrangement

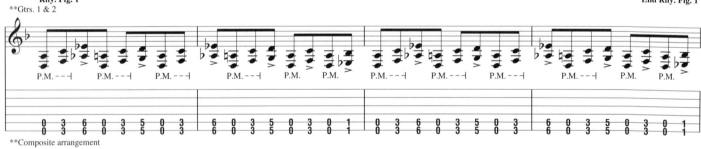

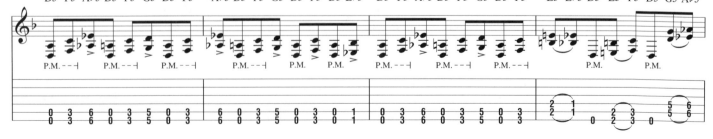

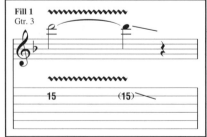

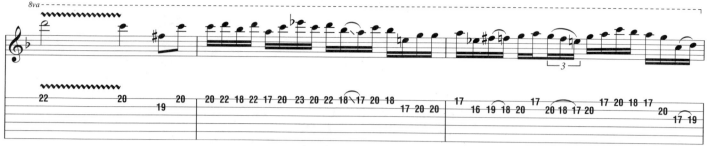

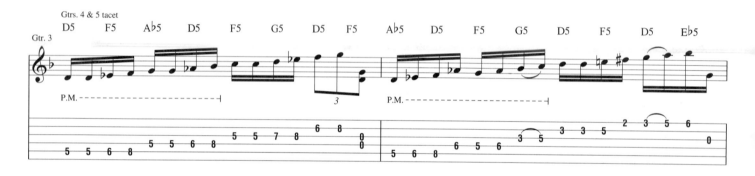

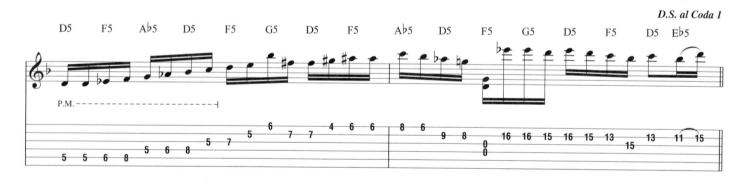

D.S. al Coda 1

Coda 1

when   all   hope ___ is

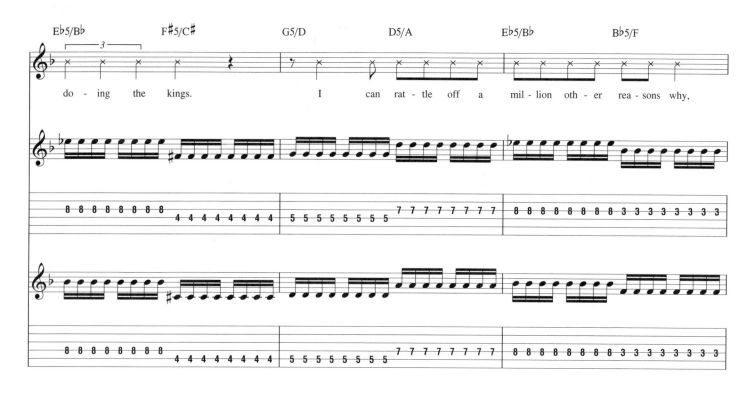

D.S. al Coda 2

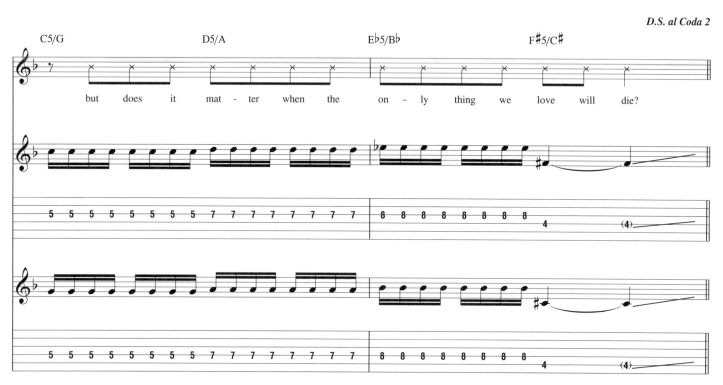

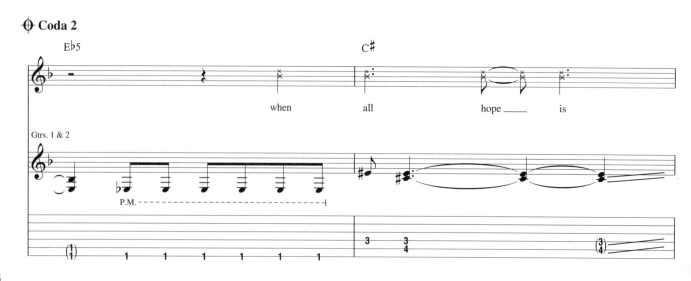

Outro